FREEDOM AND THE SELF

FREEDOM
AND THE SELF

ESSAYS ON THE PHILOSOPHY OF
DAVID FOSTER WALLACE

Edited by Steven M. Cahn and Maureen Eckert

COLUMBIA UNIVERSITY PRESS   NEW YORK

Columbia University Press
Publishers Since 1893
New York   Chichester, West Sussex
cup.columbia.edu
Copyright © 2015 Columbia University Press
All rights reserved

Library of Congress Cataloging-in-Publication Data
Freedom and the self : essays on the philosophy of David Foster Wallace /
    edited by Steven M. Cahn and Maureen Eckert.
        Pages cm
    Includes bibliographical references and index.
    ISBN 978-0-231-16152-7 (cloth : alk. paper) — ISBN 978-0-231-16153-4
(pbk. : alk. paper) — ISBN 978-0-231-53916-6 (e-book)
    1. Wallace, David Foster.   2. Fate and fatalism.   3. Taylor, Richard,
1919–2003.   4. Semantics.   I. Cahn, Steven M., editor.
    BJ1461.F77 2015
    191—dc23

                                                              2014035372

Cover images: Shutterstock
Cover design: Marc Cohen

References to websites (URLs) were accurate at the time of
writing. Neither the author nor Columbia University Press is
responsible for URLs that may have expired or changed since
the manuscript was prepared.

CONTENTS

INTRODUCTION

STEVEN M. CAHN AND MAUREEN ECKERT

L
ike Mary Ann (or Marian) Evans, better known as George Eliot, who translated Spinoza's monumental *Ethica, Ordine Geometrico Demonstrata*, and T. S. Eliot, who was offered a faculty position in the Department of Philosophy at Harvard University, David Foster Wallace (1962–2008) was a major literary figure who also excelled in philosophy.

The son of the noted philosopher James D. Wallace, who taught at the University of Illinois at Urbana-Champaign, David Foster Wallace, like his father, was graduated from Amherst College, receiving a BA degree summa cum laude in 1985 with majors in both English and philosophy. His honors thesis in English was published two years later as his first novel, *The Broom of the System*; his honors thesis in philosophy, titled "Richard Taylor's 'Fatalism' and the Semantics of Physical Modality" was published in 2011 by Columbia University Press as the centerpiece of a collection we edited titled *Fate, Time, and Language*.

The preface to that book concluded with the hope that Wallace's arguments "will be taken seriously and subjected to careful scrutiny." The original essays in this volume provide such assessments of Wallace's philosophical thought, whether in his monograph on fatalism or his other works.

Our first three contributors consider in detail Wallace's analysis of Richard Taylor's controversial 1962 essay, "Fatalism," in which

Taylor maintains that, when suitably connected, six presuppositions widely accepted by contemporary philosophers imply the fatalistic conclusion that we have no more control over future events than we have now over past ones. (Taylor's article and the spate of replies it engendered can be found in our *Fate, Time, and Language*.)

William Hasker considers the semantic system developed by Wallace to be a "splendid achievement" but doubts Wallace's claim to have demonstrated a new objection to Taylor's reasoning. Hasker, however, also believes that a contemporary philosophy of time known as eternalism, which leaves no room in the world for alternative possibilities, poses a threat to freedom, thus suggesting the importance of continuing to explore the issues that concerned Taylor and Wallace.

Gila Sher admires "the richness and inventiveness" of Wallace's work and judges that it "sets a new standard for a future defense of Taylor's argument." She believes that Wallace anticipated ideas published almost two decades later by the philosopher of logic John McFarlane, who has argued that truth depends on a context of assessment.

M. Oreste Fiocco describes Wallace's discussion as "sophisticated" and "important" but claims that, like other critics of Taylor,

Wallace failed to appreciate that Taylor's argument has the form of a reductio ad absurdum: assuming the truth of his opponents' position, showing its unacceptable consequences, and thereby demonstrating its falsity. Whereas Wallace concluded by challenging Taylor to "do metaphysics, not semantics," Fiocco responds that Taylor is offering a metaphysical argument that defends the existence of contingencies, possibilities never realized but integral to the world.

Maureen Eckert adapts Wallace's semantic System J to the issue of whether time travel is possible. Drawing additionally on the work of David Lewis, she seeks to offer an account of how any apparent contradictions in the concept of time travel can be avoided. She leaves open whether Wallace would have considered this feature of his system to be a "bug" or a positive implication.

Daniel R. Kelly asks whether Wallace was a fox or a hedgehog. Granted, he knew many things, but did his work also have a single overarching idea? Kelly finds such unity in Wallace's concern for the importance of free choice, a theme that runs throughout this collection.

Freedom requires genuine alternatives, not only in action but, most importantly to Wallace, in the exercise of "some control over *how* and *what* you think" (*This Is Water*). A valuable education provides the self with the power to choose with awareness what has meaning while "really good fiction could have as dark a worldview as it wished, but it'd find a way both to depict this world and to illuminate the possibilities for being alive and human in it" (*Review of Contemporary Fiction* 13, no. 2).

Taking the latter theme as their starting point, Nathan Ballantyne and Justin Tosi consider Wallace's view of the good life. In their discussion they refer to the work of numerous contemporary philosophers, including Richard Rorty, Galen Strawson, Christine Korsgaard, Charles Tayor, J. David Velleman, David Schmidtz, and Kurt Baier. Some may be surprised to see these names mentioned in a discussion of the thought of David Foster Wallace. Such a juxtaposition, however, would be expected by anyone who appreciates Wallace's talents as not only a writer but also a philosopher.

We are grateful to our editor, Wendy Lochner, for her guidance and encouragement, and to assistant editor Christine Dunbar for her critical role in bringing the project to fruition. We also appreciate the care provided by our manuscript editor, Robert Fellman, as well as the efforts throughout the production made by the staff at Columbia University Press. Above all, we thank the devoted scholars whose insightful contributions have made this volume possible.

FREEDOM AND THE SELF

1

DAVID FOSTER WALLACE AND
THE FALLACIES OF "FATALISM"

WILLIAM HASKER

In 1985 David Foster Wallace, then a senior at Amherst College, decided to devote his philosophy honors thesis to the issues raised by Richard Taylor's paper "Fatalism," published two decades earlier. Taylor's paper had generated a storm of discussion, most of it critical of his argument. (Apparently, no one actually considered the argument to be sound, not even Taylor.) Wallace, however, found all of the previous criticisms to be inadequate in one way or another, so he set out to provide a new refutation, creating in the process a new system of formal logic to deal with what he termed "situational physical necessity and possibility."

Now, Wallace's thesis does not by any means represent a turning point in recent philosophy; indeed, its very existence was known to only a few before its publication in the book to which this present volume is a sequel (Wallace 2011). Nevertheless, I believe there is a good deal to be learned from a reexamination of Taylor's argument, the various criticisms of it, and Wallace's response. Considering these matters can throw light not only on Taylor's and Wallace's philosophical positions but also on the general philosophical climate of the period. I will begin by presenting Taylor's argument, followed by a selection from the criticisms made of it and the reasons Taylor and Wallace, as well as Taylor's defender Steven Cahn, found them inadequate. This will be followed by a summary of Wallace's system and the criticisms of Taylor's argument that emerged from it; these criticisms are compared with those that had been made previously. Finally, I offer a few comments on the guise in which these problems present themselves in our own time.

The narrative of Taylor's argument for fatalism is best begun not with his article of that name (Taylor 1962a) but with an earlier article, "The Problem of Future Contingencies" (Taylor 1957). This was a carefully argued defense of Aristotle's view that assertions concerning future contingent events are neither true nor false; it also included a proposed revision of the traditional theological doctrine of divine omniscience. The article is well-balanced, reasonable, and contains excellent scholarship on Aristotle; furthermore, it makes a good (though perhaps not airtight) case for its conclusion. In spite of these merits, however, the article fell mostly on deaf ears, to the extent that it reached any ears at all (often a moot question concerning scholarly publications!).

The failure of this article to elicit a greater response may well have been a motivating factor for the subsequent publication, in 1962, of Taylor's essay on fatalism. The strategy of the argument (though not its explicit form) would seem to have been a kind of *reductio ad absurdum:* "If you won't accept Aristotle's and my argument concerning future contingents, see what you will be stuck with in its place!" What appeared in place of the Aristotelian conclusion was precisely fatalism, which Taylor described thus:

> A fatalist—if there is any such—thinks he cannot do anything about the future. He thinks it is not up to him what is going to happen next year, tomorrow, or the very next moment. He thinks that even his own behavior is not in the least within his power, any more than the motions of the heavenly bodies, the events of remote history, or the political developments in China. It would, accordingly, be pointless for him to deliberate about what he is

going to do, for a man deliberates only about such things as he believes are within his power to do and to forego, or to affect by his doings and foregoings.

(TAYLOR 1962A, 41)

Taylor proposed to deduce fatalism from a set of six "presuppositions made almost universally in contemporary philosophy" (Taylor 1962a, 42). I give these presuppositions in his own words, though with some omissions where nothing essential is lost thereby.

First, we presuppose that any proposition whatever is either true or, if not true, then false. . . .

Second, we presuppose that, if any state of affairs is sufficient for, though logically unrelated to, the occurrence of some further condition at the same or any other time, then the former cannot occur without the latter occurring also. This is simply the standard manner in which the concept of *sufficiency* is explicated. . . .

Third, we presuppose that, if the occurrence of any condition is necessary for, but logically unrelated to, the occurrence of some other condition at the same or any other time, then the latter cannot occur without the former occurring also. This is simply the standard manner in which the concept of a *necessary condition* is explicated. . . .

Fourth, we presuppose that, if one condition or set of conditions is sufficient for (ensures) another, then that other is necessary (essential) for it, and conversely, if one condition or set of conditions is necessary (essential) for another, then that other is sufficient for (ensures) it. This is but a logical consequence of the second and third presuppositions.

Fifth, we presuppose that no agent can perform any given act if there is lacking, at the same or any other time, some condition necessary for the occurrence of that act. This follows simply from the idea of anything being essential for the accomplishment of something else. . . .

And *sixth*, we presuppose that time is not by itself "efficacious"; that is, that the mere passage of time does not augment or diminish the capacities of anything and, in particular, that it does not enhance or decrease an agent's powers or abilities. . . .

(TAYLOR 1962A, 43–44)

Of these presuppositions, P2, P3, and P4 are essentially definitions; apart from minor quibbles, they are effectively beyond challenge. P6 is seriously ambiguous,[1] but this is not too important inasmuch as it is not actually employed as a premise in the proof Taylor offers. His own inclination is to reject P1, the assumption of bivalence; as we shall see, he had a surprise awaiting him in this territory. Much of the criticism by other philosophers, however, was centered on P5. But before getting into that, we need to look at Taylor's proof of fatalism.

Taylor takes as his example (with a tip of the hat to Aristotle) the occurrence or nonoccurrence of a naval battle on a particular day. First, he considers the situation the day *after* the naval battle either occurred or failed to occur. He assumes that

conditions are such that only if there was a naval battle yesterday does the newspaper carry a certain kind (shape) of headline—i.e., that such a battle is essential for this kind of headline—whereas if it carries a certain different sort (shape) of headline, this will ensure that there was no such battle.[2] Now, then, I am about to perform one or the other of two acts, namely, one of seeing a headline of the first kind, or one of seeing a headline of the second kind.

(TAYLOR 1962A, 44)

Now, for me to read the headline stating that no battle occurred, the nonoccurrence of a naval battle yesterday is a necessary condition.[3] And it follows from P5 that, this necessary condition being absent—that is, if a battle did in fact occur—it is *not in my power* to perform the action of reading that sort of headline. And on the other hand, for me to read the headline stating that the battle had occurred, a necessary condition is the occurrence of the battle. Once again, it follows from P5 that, if this necessary condition is absent—that is, if no battle occurred—it is not in my power to read a headline stating that the battle had occurred. So, given the situation as described, *I have no control over* which sort of headline I will be reading. Taylor goes on to say, "this conclusion is perfectly in accordance with common sense, for we all are . . . fatalists with respect to the past" (Taylor 1962a, 45). For future reference, call this *Argument I*.

Next, Taylor considers the situation the day *before* the battle would occur or fail to occur. Now we are to imagine that

> I am a naval commander, about to issue my order of the day to the fleet. We assume, further, that, within the totality of other conditions prevailing, my issuing of a certain kind of order will ensure that a naval battle will occur tomorrow, whereas if I issue another kind of order, this will ensure that no naval battle occurs.
>
> (TAYLOR 1962A, 46)

Now, my issuing an order of the first kind is sufficient (given the other conditions that prevail) for a naval battle to occur; it follows from this (by P4) that the occurrence of the battle is a *necessary condition* of my issuing such an order. But now it follows, given P5, that in the absence of this necessary condition—that is, if no battle occurs—it is *not in my power* to issue an order of that particular sort. And on the other hand, my issuing an order of the other sort is sufficient to ensure that no naval battle occurs; thus, (by P4) the *nonoccurrence* of a battle is a necessary condition of my issuing an order of this second sort. And once again it follows, given P5, that absent this necessary condition—that is, if a battle does occur—it is not in my power to issue an order of this second sort. But either it is true that a naval battle will occur, or it is true that no naval battle will occur (by P1)—and whichever of these is the case, *I have no control over* which sort of order I will issue. And this result, extended to cover each and every one of my actions, is fatalism. Call this *Argument II.*

Before we address the criticisms that were made of these arguments, it seems appropriate to call attention to some dramatic but misleading rhetoric in Taylor's article—rhetoric, I surmise, that was put in place in order to enhance the "shock effect" of his thesis and elicit a more forceful response from his readers. The conclusion of the article[4] manages to suggest, without actually stating, that Taylor either accepted fatalism or was strongly inclined in that direction, something we know was not the case. Even more egregious, however, is his initial characterization of the fatalistic hypothesis. It is already misleading to say that we have no more control over our own behavior than over the motions of the heavenly bodies. As compatibilists on free will have pointed out at great length, even if our behavior is causally determined it *is controlled* by our own desires, intentions, and decisions, something that obviously does not apply to the heavenly motions or the events of remote history. And the claim that it would be pointless for us to deliberate is simply false. People who seriously believe in fatalism (a.k.a. determinism),[5] such as theological Calvinists, are often at pains to deny that our deliberations, decisions, and exertions of effort are pointless. All of these things, they rightly point out, *make a difference in the world* because they make a difference to our actions. It's true enough that, as we consider the matter from a detached perspective, we will conclude (if we are determinists) that no other course of action was really possible. But that does not mean that our efforts are in vain. Taylor's description may capture the connotations of "fatalism" as the term is often used, but it goes far beyond anything that is warranted by the fatalistic doctrine he argues for.

At this point I propose to skip ahead a bit and address an objection to Taylor's argument that appeared at a slightly later stage in the discussion. In 1964 Steven Cahn published an article (Cahn 1964) in which he defended Taylor's argument from some of the more common objections raised against it. However, he added a new objection of his own, an objection that has the distinction of being the *only* objection that Taylor himself ever recognized as having any validity. The point made by Cahn is one that we might feel, in retrospect, ought to have been obvious all along. The fact remains, however, that for a considerable period of time it was *not* obvious, either to Taylor or to any of the highly qualified philosophers who had undertaken to refute Taylor's argument.

Here, in brief, is Cahn's point:[6] It is, as we have seen, a necessary condition of the admiral's issuing a certain order that there is a naval battle the following day. Now, suppose that, as he is considering what to do, the proposition "There will be a naval battle tomorrow" is neither true nor false. It follows from this, trivially, that "There will be a naval battle tomorrow" *is not true*, and because it is not true, a necessary condition for his issuing that order is lacking, and it follows (by P5) that no such order can be issued. On the other hand, however, it is a necessary condition of the admiral's issuing a different sort of order that there shall be no naval battle on the following day. But once again: the proposition "There will be no naval battle tomorrow" is, by hypothesis, neither true nor false. It now follows trivially that this proposition also *is not true*, and because it is not true, a necessary condition of his issuing that other sort of order is lacking, and it follows (by P5) that he cannot issue this kind of order either.

This argument is easily generalized to arrive at the conclusion that, on the assumption that future contingent propositions are neither true nor false, it is never possible for any person to perform any action whatsoever. But this conclusion is not merely repugnant (as many find fatalism to be) but very obviously false and absurd.

Now, in one way Cahn's objection actually strengthens Taylor's argument, by showing that it does not depend on a premise (namely, P1) that it had formerly seemed to depend on. However, the objection creates a severe problem for Taylor. Undoubtedly his original motivation for the argument was to support the Aristotelian conclusion that future contingent propositions lack classical truth values. But now it appears that rejecting classical truth values for future contingents not merely fails to avoid the fatalistic conclusion but in fact makes things a great deal worse. The upshot is that Taylor is still confronted with his own argument for fatalism, but with no apparent way to escape from the argument's conclusion. In a response to Cahn's article, Taylor states, "I feel obliged to concede . . . that it may be quite unhelpful to try modifying the traditional interpretation of the law of excluded middle. Perhaps some of my other presuppositions are doubtful, but I can imagine no reason for rejecting any of them other than the one so frequently brought forth; namely, that they seem to have fatalistic implications" (Taylor 1964, 110). Nevertheless, Taylor did not abandon his argument but continued to include it, in an altered form, in the next edition of his *Metaphysics*.[7] It may be that Taylor came to regard his argument as a conundrum—a philosophical puzzle for which a solution is required, but for which none seems to be available.[8] On the other hand, the way the argument is discussed in the second edition of *Metaphysics* could lead one to think that by 1974 Taylor had come to embrace fatalism or at least to consider its truth as a strong possibility.[9]

We now turn to the objection concerning which Taylor said that it "is so familiar that I have come to anticipate it every time I hear this discussed" (Taylor 1962b, 57). Taylor credits John Turk Saunders for having stated the objection best, so we shall begin with Saunders's statement. He wrote:

> Taylor errs . . . in supposing that no agent has within his power an act for which a necessary condition is lacking. I suspect that he is led to make this supposition by equivocal reasoning of the following sort. He sees that (1) no agent can perform an act if a necessary condition for that act is lacking. But this means only that (2) as a matter of logic, if condition x is necessary for the occurrence of act y and x is lacking, then no agent performs y. The expression "can" functions only to indicate that the consequent of the second formulation follows logically from its antecedent. Taylor may then have equivocated with respect to "can," taking it this time to mean the same as "has the power to." In this way he may have become convinced that no agent has the power to perform an act if a necessary condition for that act is lacking.
>
> (SAUNDERS 1962, 54)

Saunders then argues that this supposition of Taylor's is erroneous:

> My knocking upon a thin wooden door with my fist is a sufficient condition for the door's shaking. Hence the door's shaking is a necessary condition for my knocking upon the door. But the door's shaking is not a necessary condition for my *ability* to knock upon the door. (If it were, then my mere ability to knock upon the door would suffice to make it shake.) I may decide not to knock and the door may not shake, but it does not follow that I did not have it in my power to knock.
>
> (SAUNDERS 1962, 54)

He goes on to say,

> Now we may solve (or dissolve) Taylor's problem by noting that he is not entitled to conclude: Either it is not within my power to issue order O [the order that would lead to the naval battle], or it is not within my power to issue order O'. The occurrence of a naval battle on the morrow is a necessary condition of O but not of the ability to issue O; and the non-occurrence of a naval battle on the morrow is a necessary condition of O' but not of the ability to issue O'. (To suppose otherwise, as Taylor does, is to adopt a position which logically implies that my *ability* to issue O is a sufficient condition for a naval battle on the morrow and that my *ability* to issue O is a sufficient condition for the nonoccurrence of a naval battle on the morrow.)
>
> (SAUNDERS 1962, 55)

This reasoning is apparently straightforward, but the dialectical situation is really quite complex. On the face of it, Saunders is rejecting Taylor's premise P5, which states that "no agent can perform any given act if there is lacking . . . some condition necessary for the occurrence of that act." His reason for doing so is that this premise violates the ordinary usage of language, by understanding "I have the power to do y" as entailing "I do y," when the expression "have the power," as ordinarily used, has no such entailment.[10] Now, this may seem to invite the response (which was actually offered by Taylor—see Taylor 1964, 107) that the assertion that I have the power to do y if and only if I actually do y is simply the fatalistic doctrine itself. It seems, then, that Saunders's objection to Taylor's argument amounts to pointing out that the argument has fatalism as its conclusion. But of course that is precisely Taylor's point, so this does not seem to amount to much as an objection.

To respond to Saunders in this way, however, overlooks an important element in the situation, namely that Taylor's argument is supposed to be based on *"presuppositions made almost universally in contemporary philosophy"* (Taylor 1962a, 42). Now presumably philosophers who make those presuppositions intend, in making them, to be using language in the normal, everyday way, not in some special way that is peculiar to fatalism. So if the presuppositions, the premises of Taylor's argument, require such peculiar uses of language to be adjudged as true, this is an excellent reason for rejecting his claim that these presuppositions are almost universally made.

How might Taylor respond to this point? On the face of it, two types of answer seem to be possible. One might, on the one hand, argue that the way the presuppositions are understood by Taylor does indeed correspond to normal usage, albeit a different usage than the one Saunders takes to be normative. Or, one might provide an independent argument showing that philosophers must, on pain of irrationality, accept Taylor's premises as they stand, whether or not this involves a deviation from standard usage. (This assumes, to be sure, that standard usage may at times be involved in confusions and contradictions.) If Taylor can do either or both of these things, he can rebut Saunders's charge that his position is based on fallacious reasoning. As it turns out, Taylor avails himself of both types of responses.

Taylor admits that Saunders's point is correct with regard to "the usual sense of ability, which consists in having the skill strength, equipment, or knowing how" (Taylor 1962b, 57). However, he believes that there is another sense of ability that is relevant. Now, Taylor is certainly right in contending that there is more than one sense of "ability" that may be relevant here. Take the situation that concerns one's ability to read a headline in today's paper. We ask the person whether he is now able to read a headline stating that there has been a naval battle. One perfectly understandable and sensible response might be, "Of course! My eyes are just fine, the light is adequate, and I am fully able to read any headline whatever." Or, he might respond, "Well, I can't do that *now*, because I have seen today's paper and there is no such headline." The second response, unlike the first, uses "able" in a sense that takes into account the *circumstances* in which the person finds himself—circumstances that preclude his being able to read *that sort* of headline. And now we ask the admiral on that same day (the day after the battle would have occurred), "Were you able, the day before yesterday, to give your ships order O?" He might reply, "Of course I was able! I am entrusted with full authority to command the fleet, and if I chose to give such an order I could certainly have done it." Or, he might conceivably reply, "Actually I couldn't give such an order the day before yesterday, because my ships were not in the initial positions they would need to be in for such an order to be executed." Here again, the second reply understands "ability" in a way that takes account of circumstances. So far, so good. But suppose the admiral were to say, "No, I was completely incapable of giving such an order. For if I had given that order, there would have been a naval battle yesterday, and as you can see, there was no such battle." In that case, I think we would have to conclude that the admiral was joking—or perhaps, that he had taken up philosophy! I trust the point is clear: while there is indeed more than one sense of "ability," there does not seem to be any ordinary sense of that word in which this latter statement on the part of the admiral would make sense. But that is what would be needed for Taylor's premise P5 to pass muster before the bar of ordinary language.

However that may be, Taylor has another arrow in his quiver. He quotes Saunders's argument (given above) about knocking on a thin wooden door, which concludes that "I may decide not to knock and the door may not shake, but it does not follow that I did not have it in my power to knock." Taylor replies, "This is initially most persuasive, but to see how it fails, we need only to produce the same argument to show that I have it within my power to make something happen in the past which did not happen. Thus,

> My reading a certain kind of headline is a sufficient condition for there being a naval battle yesterday. Hence there being a naval battle yesterday is a necessary condition for my reading such a headline. But the occurrence of such a battle is not a necessary condition for my ability to read such a headline. (If it were, then my mere ability to read such a headline would suffice to make the naval battle occur yesterday.) I may decide not to read such a headline and the battle may not have occurred yesterday, but it does not follow that I do not have it in my power to read such a headline.

> Now if Saunders's argument against my fatalism is a good one, this argument refutes fatalism with respect to the past, for it is the *same* argument, with only a difference of tenses. But this argument obviously does not refute fatalism with respect to the past, nor does Saunders's argument refute it with respect to the future.

(TAYLOR 1962B, 59)

Saunders, however, was unconvinced by this. Here is his rejoinder:

> Taylor wrongly takes me to argue that, even though a door does not shake, I did have it in my power to make it shake (by knocking upon it). This leads him to say that the same sort of argument will show that I have it in my power to make something happen in the past even though it did not happen. But I argued, not that I *did* have it in my power to make the door shake, but only that it *does not follow from* the door's not shaking that I did not have

the power to make it shake. Thus I am not thereby committed to arguing that I have the power to make an event happen in the past. Let me, then, rephrase Taylor's charge so that it *will* apply to my position: if the non-occurrence of an event in the future does not entail my lack of power to bring about that event, then neither does the non-occurrence of an event in the past entail my lack of power to bring about that event. So phrased, I must say that I agree, at any rate to this extent: it is not due to the non-occurrence of an event in the past that I lack the power to bring about that event.

(SAUNDERS 1962, 67)

In his defense of Taylor, Steven Cahn notes Taylor's contention that "if Saunders's argument does indeed refute fatalism in respect to the future, then it also refutes fatalism in respect to the past." He then cites Saunders's reply (quoted above) but says, "this does not at all seem to refute Taylor's charge. . . . Is there some actual difference between the past and the future which would account for making this distinction? If Saunders wishes to answer Taylor's charge he must point out such a difference, for it is the denial of such a difference upon which Taylor's argument essentially rests" (Cahn 1964, 99–100).

As Cahn correctly observes, Taylor is challenging Saunders to point out some relevant difference between what we have termed Argument I, which establishes fatalism concerning the past, and Argument II, which establishes fatalism concerning the future. And Cahn is right: Saunders offers no such difference. But what Cahn apparently fails to see is that Saunders has a different response to Taylor's challenge. Rather than providing a way to distinguish between Argument I and Argument II, Saunders concludes that *both* arguments are unsound. (Apparently he is well advised to do so, since he rejects Taylor's premise P5, which is an essential part of both arguments.) Saunders says, furthermore, that he *is not concerned*, in his argument against Taylor, *either* to refute *or* to establish "fatalism concerning the past"—nor, for that matter, is he concerned to refute fatalism concerning the future. What he is concerned to do is to refute *Taylor's argument* for fatalism concerning the future, and this he is satisfied has been successfully done. If the question were to arise, why we cannot bring about past events, some other approach would be required.[11] An important point concerning this exchange, by the way, is that both Taylor and Cahn seem to assume that Taylor's opponents must undertake the task of *refuting fatalism*—that is, of establishing that we do in fact have free will in the sense in which the fatalist denies this. But of course, this is an enormous task; the controversy has already raged for two millennia and shows little sign of abating. Fortunately, the opponent of Taylor's argument need do no such thing. For an opponent such as Saunders, the task is merely one of *refuting that argument*—a task Saunders takes himself to have successfully performed.

Nevertheless, Cahn can still argue that Taylor's opponents need to provide some explanation for the difference in the *apparent cogency* of the two arguments. "The power of Taylor's approach is that the first argument seems acceptable until the second argument is produced. Then the first argument loses its appeal" (Cahn, private communication). This does seem to be a relevant challenge; I propose to meet it by elaborating slightly Saunders's example of knocking on a door. This example will also help us see more clearly why Taylor's premise P5 is defective. So here is the example: You and Saunders together came to visit a friend's apartment, and Saunders pushed the doorbell button several times with no response. He turned away in disappointment, and you followed him out of the building. But then it occurred to you to ask, "Don't you think you ought to have tried knocking on the door?

I didn't hear the doorbell actually ring; it may not be working." He responds, "No, I was quite unable to knock on the door. For a necessary condition of my knocking on the door is that the door should shake—and as you could see, it did not shake the whole time we were there." Of course this statement is absurd, but why is it absurd? A very little reflection should reveal the reason: *Although the door did not in fact shake, it was fully within Saunders's power to make it shake, simply by knocking on it.* And this suggests the needed revision to P5: "No agent can perform any given act if there is lacking, at the same or any other time, some condition necessary for the occurrence of that act, *unless it is also in the agent's power to bring about that necessary condition.*" It is, I think, completely obvious that this, rather than the original P5, is the correct principle—but this principle will fail entirely to yield Taylor's fatalistic conclusion. Furthermore, the expanded example helps us understand why Taylor can make his (specious) claim that P5 is almost universally accepted. If we are inclined to accept it, this is because we do not ordinarily think of something like the door's shaking as a *condition* of someone's knocking on it (even though it is that, given Taylor's definition of "necessary condition"). Rather, we would think of the door's shaking as a *consequence* of the knocking. The "almost universal acceptance," insofar as it obtains at all, is based on an understanding of P5 that is different than the one Taylor requires for his argument.

At this point considerations of space prompt us to move on, leaving undiscussed many more twists and turns in the debate over Taylor's argument. So we turn to Wallace's evaluation of the debate and of the objections to Taylor that had appeared in the literature. His comments on those objections occupy only a small part of his thesis, but they are significant because they have a bearing on his claim to have offered new objections that are more successful than those made previously. Many of his remarks echo replies already offered by Taylor and by Cahn, but one point that calls for special mention[12] is Wallace's diagnosis of (what he takes to be) the failure of Saunders's objections.

It is important to see why Saunders' seemingly plausible objections do not really succeed in refuting the fatalist. They amount to the claim that Taylor's argument has implications which go against our intuitions about the world and about language. But see that the fatalist does not share our intuitions. He has metaphysical intuitions of his own about the way the world operates and the way language ought to be used to characterize those operations. He also has an *argument* for his intuitions here, Taylor's. Because intuitions are obviously not refutations, mere claims that the premises or conclusion of the Taylor argument has counterintuitive implications or requires counterintuitive reasoning of some sort cannot by themselves refute the argument.

(WALLACE 2011, 155).

Unfortunately, this passage contains multiple confusions of the sort we have already seen in previous answers to objections. First of all, it is not at all incumbent on the critic to *refute fatalism*—that is, to show that fatalism is false. The critic's task is merely to *refute Taylor's argument*. Intuitions can very well contribute to this in a major way, by showing that the near-universal agreement claimed by Taylor for his premises is a sham; in order to arrive at his conclusion, he must understand the premises in a different way than any that would be acceptable to the philosophers he is claiming in support. Furthermore, Taylor's argument has force in overruling the intuitive objections *only if* the argument is based on premises that really can claim widespread acceptance. But some of the objections show that it is very doubtful that such a claim can be made on behalf of the premises *as Taylor understands them*.

However this may be, Wallace is very clear about the nature of his own response to Taylor:

> where most have tried to justify [their] rejection by disallowing one or more of the presuppositions that serve as the explicit or implicit premises of Taylor's argument, here I am going to try to bend over backwards to accept Taylor's premises, to grant him everything he seems to want in the argument, and then to show that the conclusion he desires still does not follow validly from that argument. This is the project in outline.
>
> (WALLACE 2011, 151)

This is admirably explicit; we need to see how the plan is executed. The core of Wallace's response to Taylor consists in a formal logical system, "System J," which was devised in order to address situations such as those involved in Taylor's argument for fatalism. It should be said that System J was not a solitary accomplishment on Wallace's part. He consulted extensively in setting it up, but clearly the initiative and most of the energy and effort came from Wallace.[13] There is not the space here for a full treatment of System J (that would require an entire article by itself), but I will try to give enough of an account of it to enable the reader to see how it addresses Taylor's argument.

The purpose of System J is to give an account of "physical-modal" propositions; crucially, these propositions speak about what is physically possible or impossible *at a time, given the physical situation as it obtains at that time.* (It is assumed that the laws of nature are those that hold in our actual world.) Wallace illustrates the difference between this sort of modality and other kinds with a series of examples: "It is not possible for me to be both a human being and a quartz crystal"—this is logical impossibility. "It is not possible for me to travel faster than the speed of light"—this is physical impossibility simpliciter. "It is not possible for me, now in Champaign, Illinois, to be touching a building in Massachusetts thirty seconds from now"—this is physical impossibility *given the constraints of time and situation* (Wallace 2011, 149). It is this latter sort of modality with which System J is concerned, and the familiar "□" and "◊," as used here, will be taken to refer to this sort of modality.[14] A typical proposition of System J has the form "$t_m ◊ t_n$ E," where E designates a kind of event, and "m" and "n" are temporal indices; the proposition states that "At t_m it is possible that E occurs at t_n." It is important that "n" and "m" may have either the same or different values; this is because the truth value of "◊ t_n E" may vary, *depending on the time at which the possibility in question is evaluated.* Once again, Wallace offers a helpful pair of examples:

> In "It couldn't rain last night; last night a high-pressure ridge was keeping all rain-clouds away," we are evaluating the modal character of rain-last-night in light of the conditions we know to have obtained last night. But in "It can't have rained last night; there are no puddles on the sidewalk this morning," we are evaluating the modal character of rain-last-night quite obviously in light of the puddle-free conditions we know to obtain now.
>
> (WALLACE 2011, 173)

It is important to realize that only the first of these two sentences says anything about whether or not rain was possible *last night.*

Wallace develops his case against Taylor by setting out what he terms the "Taylor Inequivalence" (Wallace 2011, 159), an inequivalence between two propositions that can be symbolized as follows:

(A) $\quad t_2 \sim ◊t_1\, O$

(B) $\quad t_1 \sim ◊t_1\, O$

Here "O" represents the event of the admiral's giving order O (the order that would result in a naval battle),[15] t_1 is the time immediately before such an order would have been issued, and t_2 is a time the following afternoon, when the battle, had it occurred, would have been in progress. So the two propositions, spelled out in English, are as follows:

(A′)   As of t_2, it is impossible that order O is given at t_1.

(B′)   As of t_1, it is impossible that order O is given at t_1.

Now, Wallace makes three claims about these two propositions. *First*, the two propositions are not equivalent: (B) entails (A) but not vice versa. *Second*, what Taylor needs for his argument is (B); (A) does not suffice. But *third*, only (A) can be properly derived, so Taylor's argument fails. I believe Wallace is correct in all three claims. (A) describes the situation as we "look back" from the afternoon of the second day, when no battle has occurred. We conclude, quite properly, that it cannot be the case that the admiral gave order O on the previous day, because if he had done so there would be a battle in progress, and there is no such battle. But this apparently has no bearing on the admiral's *power or ability* to give such an order at t_1. (B), on the other hand, describes the situation *at t_1* and asserts that *at that time* it was impossible for order O to be given—but if that *was* impossible, then the admiral lacked the power or ability to give such an order, which is precisely the fatalistic conclusion. If we follow Wallace's discussion of the situation (which on the whole is quite persuasive), I believe we will conclude that he has established his three claims. Furthermore, the same result can be derived more formally from the full, "official" exposition of System J (Wallace 2011, 190–198), which for reasons of space we can't go into here.[16]

So far, then, Wallace is doing well. But what of his claim that his objection to Taylor is successful where others have not been? Or his claim that, rather than contesting Taylor's premises, he has granted the premises and shown the argument to be invalid? The first thing to notice is that the "Taylor Inequivalence" is extremely similar to the objection first posed by Saunders. According to Saunders, we recall, Taylor

> sees that (1) no agent can perform an act if a necessary condition for that act is lacking. But this means only that (2) as a matter of logic, if condition x is necessary for the occurrence of act y and x is lacking, then no agent performs y.

This corresponds closely to proposition (A): Since no sea battle has occurred, we conclude that it cannot be the case that the admiral gave order O. However, Saunders goes on,

> Taylor may then have equivocated with respect to "can," taking it this time to mean the same as "has the power to." In this way he may have become convinced that no agent has the power to perform an act if a necessary condition for that act is lacking.

This conclusion, which Saunders takes to have been illegitimately inferred, is essentially the same as proposition (B), which states that *at the time when the order would have been given* it was impossible for such an order to be given and therefore not in the admiral's power to give it. The two objections are, if not strictly equivalent, nearly enough so as to make little difference.

Now, if Wallace's objection and the one offered by Saunders are virtually the same, Wallace can claim to have succeeded where Saunders failed only if he has some new, decisive support for his objection that was not provided by Saunders. And indeed, he seems to think that this is the case. With respect to a "physical-possibility-structure diagram" on p. 186, he claims that it "allows us to justify this claim [viz., about the Taylor Inequivalence] in something more than an intuitive way" (Wallace 2011, 187). Is Wallace correct in this claim? In one way, he is. Certainly the diagram in question and System J as a whole flesh out the objection to Taylor's argument in a way that Saunders never did. However, Wallace may be overlooking the point that *formal logical systems rest on intuitive foundations.* At least, this is true of the systems we seriously rely upon to guide our thinking. If we couldn't see intuitively that modus ponens is a valid form of inference whereas affirming the consequent is invalid, we would have no basis for using the propositional calculus as a guide in our reasoning. And the same is true of System J; Wallace's explanation of and advocacy for System J rely heavily on examples in which he appeals to our logical intuitions. So while that system does a good deal to work out systematically the sort of reasoning involved in the objection to Taylor's argument, it by no means manages to escape from the ultimate reliance on intuition. But perhaps System J is *more effective* in spelling out those intuitions and enforcing their consequences? This may possibly be so; whether Taylor would have been convinced, had he been able to study System J, must remain an unanswered question.

To this extent, then, Wallace's claim to have succeeded where others had failed must be left unresolved. However, the same cannot be said about his other claim, to have granted Taylor's premises and shown that the argument is nevertheless invalid. In his extensive discussions it is entirely clear that he has failed to grant Taylor's premise P5 *in the sense in which Taylor understood it* (Wallace 2011, 168–170). In fact, if we grant that premise Taylor's argument can easily be shown to be valid—though in the end this does him little good, since the premise so understood is false.[17]

How then shall we assess Wallace's response to Taylor's argument? On the one hand, his creation of System J, and his articulation of his reply to Taylor in terms of that system, must be recognized as a splendid achievement, one that is not diminished by the help he received in formulating that system. (Any philosopher attempting such a task, of whatever training and experience, would be well advised to confer and consult with colleagues in the process.) On the other hand, his claim to have pointed out a fundamentally new objection, quite different from those made previously, and his claim to have granted Taylor's premises and shown his argument to be invalid cannot be sustained. But there is one more thing for which he deserves credit: he realized, in the end (Wallace 2011, 212–213), that the real project was not to "refute fatalism" but simply to turn back Taylor's argument; there remains the opportunity, for Taylor and other fatalists, to present a different sort of argument for fatalism should they choose to do so.

What does all this tell us about the overall philosophical climate during the years when Taylor's argument was being debated? Probably a number of things, but what stands out to me is the lack of a developed practice of modal reasoning. That is not to say that philosophers were unaware of the notions of possibility, necessity, contingency, and the like; of course they were aware of such things. But in those years of the 1960s, philosophy was just beginning to rid itself of the graveclothes of logical positivism, and modal reasoning was far from the center of attention. It was widely assumed that the only respectable notion of necessity was that of analyticity—and Quine, notoriously, did a great deal to undermine even analyticity. The classic work on modal logic by C. I. Lewis was already available, but modal reasoning did not enter the mainstream philosophical dialogue until about 1970, through the work of Kripke and others. (Wallace cites Kripke and Montague in developing his own system—see Wallace 2011, 177–182.) Wallace was very much on target when he concluded that a detailed, explicit treatment of the relevant sort of modality was called for, even if, in the end, he only systematized notions that others had previously put forward in a more inchoate, less systematic form.

What has become of these topics today, a quarter-century after Wallace's thesis? Taylor-style arguments for fatalism do not seem to be much in evidence, but in other respects the issues raised here remain very much alive. The question of truth values for future contingents comes to the fore in the context of the philosophy of time known as presentism: what exists (at any given time) is what exists *now*, and the truth-makers for future contingent propositions *do not exist*. Furthermore, insofar as the states of affairs are genuinely contingent, it *is not yet decided* whether these truth makers will exist or not. For this reason J. R. Lucas termed such propositions "valedictory truths"—they can be recognized as such only retrospectively, from the standpoint of a later time when the events either have or have not occurred. Many have concluded that such peculiar "truths" as these do not deserve the name, and they have opted for truth-value gaps where future contingents are concerned.[18]

On the other hand, the philosophy of time known as eternalism or four-dimensionalism (also the "stasis theory") offers the prospect of a revival of fatalism. According to this view, all the events of all times coexist in the four-dimensional spacetime continuum, and there is no such thing as a privileged present moment that is "now." The four-dimensional continuum by definition cannot change; such change as exists consists in the fact that different states of affairs obtain at different temporal indices within the continuum. It would certainly seem (though this is sometimes contested) that, on this view, there is no room for the "alternative possibilities" that are essential for free will as understood by Taylor, Wallace, and in general by advocates of libertarian free will. Four-dimensionalism, then, offers the fatalist everything she needs; no further argument is required. The threat of fatalism has by no means gone away.

NOTES

My thanks to Steven Cahn for his assistance at a number of points during the preparation of this paper. He is not, of course, responsible for my conclusions or for my remaining mistakes.

1. Raziel Abelson (1963, 79) gives a "minimalist" interpretation of P6, as asserting "the atemporality of the laws of nature." On a maximalist interpretation, P6 implies that an occurrence can just as well be rendered impossible by a *later* event as by an *earlier* event—an explicitly fatalist implication. And there are other possibilities.

2. Clearly, allowing the claims here concerning necessary and sufficient conditions requires a bit of idealization. We are to assume, among other things, that there is zero probability of a breakdown of the presses, as well as a zero probability that some misguided humorist will print up a paper with a fake headline as a practical joke. Such idealizations will typically be required in the examples used; in general we will let them pass without notice.

3. To save space, I am paraphrasing Taylor's argument here; the reader may be assured that I do not distort his intent or the logic of the argument.

4. "Apart from subjective feelings of our power to control things, there seem to be no good philosophical reasons against this opinion, and very strong ones in its favor" Taylor 1962a, 51).

5. A reader of the manuscript correctly points out that fatalism is often distinguished from determinism, with fatalism involving some additional consequences that are not implied by determinism as such. Taylor's argument, however, is really an argument for determinism, so for purposes of this essay I treat the two as equivalent. (As the text points out, Taylor in his rhetoric invokes some of the connotations of "fatalism" that are by no means supported by his argument.)

6. Once again, in order to save space I am omitting Cahn's elegant and precise formal presentation of his objection, which can be found in Cahn (1964, 103–105).

7. See Taylor (1963, 1974). There is a striking difference in the presentation of the argument for fatalism in the two editions. The first edition follows closely the exposition in the original article and points to the rejection

of P1 (bivalence) as the most promising way to escape from the fatalistic conclusion. The exposition of the argument is quite different in the second edition, where Taylor describes the rejection of bivalence as an "arbitrary fiction, resorted to for no other reason than to be rid of the detested doctrine of fatalism" (1974, 70). It may be, however, that in the second edition Taylor was being deliberately provocative, in an attempt to draw the reader into the argument and that his apparently favorable view of fatalism does not reflect his considered opinion.

8. Cahn (1967, 86n) proposed a revision of Taylor's P5 that, he claimed, avoids the difficulty stated by Cahn and still allows Taylor's argument for fatalism to go through. Taylor never responded to this suggestion, and it was never considered by Wallace, so it will not be discussed further here.

9. "We shall say, therefore, of whatever happens, that it was going to be that way. And this is a comfort, both in fortune and in adversity. We shall say of him who turns out bad and mean, that he was going to; of him who turns out happy and blessed, that he was going to; neither praising nor berating fortune, crying over what has been, lamenting what was going to be, or passing moral judgments" (Taylor 1974, 71). Wallace does not seem to have considered the version of the argument in the second edition.

10. Later on, Saunders states, "[Taylor's] position amounts to nothing more than the suggestion that we cease to use 'in one's power' in the ordinary ways, and begin to use it in his way. . . . Taylor has, in effect, recommended that we add a meaning rule to those which already govern 'in one's power,' *viz.* the rule: if it is in one's power to bring about the situation then that situation occurs" (1962, 66).

11. Saunders gives what is apparently his own answer to the question: "I have no such power because we so use our language that it is false or nonsense to say that one has the power to bring about any event whatever in the past" (1962, 67). Whether this answer is adequate will not be discussed here.

12. There is one other point that perhaps deserves passing mention, since it may account for Wallace's belief that he has shown Saunders's objection to Taylor's argument to be unsuccessful. Referencing pp. 64–66 of *Metaphysics*, Wallace states, "Taylor maintains that the occurrence of the battle tomorrow is obviously a necessary condition only of my giving the order today, not of my having the ability to give the order today, for,

were the latter true, my mere ability to give the order today would by itself be a sufficient condition for the occurrence of the battle tomorrow, which looks to be absurd" (2011, 152). Now, if Taylor had indeed said this, that would constitute a major blunder on his part because it would immediately render his argument invalid. The mistake, however, is Wallace's; no statement can be found on those pages supporting the attribution of this view to Taylor. (Perhaps Wallace was misled by a passage in which the view is attributed by Taylor to his opponents.)

13. The chief collaborator was Jay Garfield, then on the faculty of Hampshire College, who was asked by Willem de Vries, Wallace's thesis advisor, to confer with Wallace. Here in part is Garfield's description of their meetings: "It is hard at this point to say with any certainty who introduced what ideas into those conversations, and would probably have been difficult to do so at the time. These were discussions among colleagues, not ordinary supervision meetings between teacher and student. . . . I am pretty sure, but not positive, that I proposed system J and the broad sketch of its semantics (that is probably the reason David calls it J); I am also pretty sure, and a little more positive, that as soon as I did, David ran with it and showed both how it solved the central problem of demonstrating the invalidity of Taylor's argument . . . and how treating time and physical modality this way makes sense of a number of other puzzles about physical modality and time. His philosophical instincts were sure; his thought was precise. The thesis came together in a matter of a few weeks" (Garfield 2011).

14. In *Fate, Time, and Language* "□" and "◊" are printed with a strikethrough to distinguish them from other sorts of modalities. In this essay they will be used *only* to refer to Wallace's physical modalities, so there will be no ambiguity.

15. Wallace develops a new example of his own, concerning a group of terrorists who might or might not detonate a nuclear device on the Amherst College campus. For present purposes, I think it is simpler to stay with Taylor's original example.

16. There is an error in the semantic rules for System J, as printed on p. 191 in the first printing of *Fate, Time, and Language*. In Rule 2, the two disjunction signs ("∨") need to be replaced with conjunction signs ("∧"), and the same should be done with the one disjunction sign in Rule 4. Rule 2, written out in English, says in effect: "At t_n, it is possible that p is true at t_m if and only if there is a causal path j_x and a world W′ such that

W (the actual world) at t_n lies on j_x OR W′ at t_m lies on j_x OR p is true in W′ at t_m." Rule 4 says, "At t_n, p will be true in the future if and only if there is a causal path j_x OR there is a time t_m such that W (the actual world) at t_n lies on j_x and W at t_m lies on j_x and t_m is later than t_n and p is true in W at t_m." In each case, it is evident that "OR" needs to be replaced with "AND" for the rules to make sense. (I have been informed by Steven Cahn that the errors do not occur in Wallace's original manuscript. The mistakes were printer's errors and were corrected in the e-book version and in all subsequent printings.)

17. Wallace's mistake here may be attributable to his misreading of Taylor's remarks in *Metaphysics*; see note 12 above.

18. This question has attracted interest especially among the adherents of "open theism," a movement in philosophical theology that seriously embraces a revised conception of divine omniscience similar to the one suggested by Taylor in his 1957 article. (The movement is not, however, directly indebted to Taylor.) For discussion, see Tuggy (2007) and Rhoda (2011).

REFERENCES

Abelson, Raziel. 1963. "Taylor's Fatal Fallacy." *Philosophical Review* 72, no. 1. Reprinted in Cahn and Eckert 2011, 79–83. Citations refer to the reprint.

Cahn, Steven. 1964. "Fatalistic Arguments." *Journal of Philosophy* 61, no. 10. Reprinted in Cahn and Eckert 2011, 93–106. Citations refer to the reprint.

——. 1967. *Fate, Logic, and Time*. New Haven, Conn.: Yale University Press, 1967.

Cahn, S., and M. Eckert, eds. 2011. *Fate, Time, and Language: An Essay on Free Will*, by David Foster Wallace. New York: Columbia University Press.

Garfield, Jay. 2011. "David Foster Wallace as Student: A Memoir." In Cahn and Eckert 2011, 219–221.

Rhoda, Alan R. 2011. "The Fivefold Openness of the Future." In *God in an Open Universe: Science, Metaphysics, and Open Theism*, ed. William Hasker et al., 69–93. Eugene, Ore.: Pickwick.

Saunders, John Turk. 1962a. "Fatalism and Linguistic Reform." *Analysis* 23, no. 2. Reprinted in Cahn and Eckert 2011, 65–68. Citations refer to the reprint.

——. 1962b. "Professor Taylor on Fatalism." *Analysis* 23, no. 1. Reprinted in Cahn and Eckert 2011, 53–55. Citations refer to the reprint.

——. 1965. "Fatalism and Ordinary Language." *Journal of Philosophy* 62, no. 8. Reprinted in Cahn and Eckert 2011, 111–126. Citations refer to the reprint.

Taylor, Richard. 1957. "The Problem of Future Contingencies." *Philosophical Review* 66, no. 1. Reprinted as an appendix to Cahn and Eckert 2011, 223–252. Citations refer to the reprint.

——. 1962a. "Fatalism." *Philosophical Review* 71, no. 1. Reprinted in Cahn and Eckert 2011, 41–51. Citations refer to the reprint.

——. 1962b. "Fatalism and Ability." *Analysis* 23, no. 2. Reprinted in Cahn and Eckert 2011, 57–59. Citations refer to the reprint.

——. 1963. *Metaphysics*. Englewood Cliffs, N.J.: Prentice-Hall.

——. 1964. "Comment." *Journal of Philosophy* 61, no. 10. Reprinted in Cahn and Eckert 2011, 107–110. Citations refer to the reprint.

——. 1974. *Metaphysics*. 2nd ed. Englewood Cliffs, N.J.: Prentice-Hall.

Tuggy, Dale. 2007. "Three Roads to Open Theism." *Faith and Philosophy* 24, no. 1: 28–51.

Wallace, D. F. 2011. "Richard Taylor's 'Fatalism' and the Semantics of Physical Modality." In Cahn and Eckert 2011, 141–216.

2

WALLACE, FREE CHOICE, AND FATALISM

GILA SHER

In a 2005 commencement address David Foster Wallace extolled the value of "freedom of choice." But the freedom of choice he extolled was *not* the *freedom to do things in the world*, change the world, build something new in the world. The choice he talked about, the "real freedom," "the kind that is most precious," was the *freedom to choose* "*what to think*" (my italics)—the "total freedom of choice regarding what to think about." It was the freedom of "choosing to . . . alter . . . or get . . . free of [our] natural, hard-wired default setting," choosing "what you pay attention to and . . . how you construct meaning from experience," the freedom *not* to follow your "natural default setting . . . , the automatic way . . . [we] experience . . . adult life." Specifically, he said, it is "the boring, frustrating, crowded parts of adult life" "where the work of choosing is gonna come in . . . , the traffic jams and crowded aisles and long checkout lines" where you need to "make a conscious decision about how to think and what to pay attention to." "The only thing that's capital-T True is that you get to decide how you're gonna try to see" the "petty, frustrating" stuff in everyday life (Wallace 2005).

Now, of course, for a novelist to see the world in a new way is (potentially) to change the world. But in his 2005 address Wallace focused on how, in order to cope with life, we have to decide actively to see it in ways that will not let it crush us. As a way of life, this might be viewed as a strand of stoicism, yet theoretically, the view that *we cannot change reality, we can only change the way we think about it* is, in a way, a form of *fatalism*.

Twenty years earlier Wallace, then a senior at Amherst College, wrote an honors thesis (Wallace 1985) about a broader kind of freedom, a freedom that does encompass *doing things in the world*, physically changing the world. Fatalism says that "human beings, agents, have no control over what is going to happen" (144),[1] and Wallace sought to refute a controversial yet hard to unravel argument supporting this position. This argument supported fatalism in a rather unusual way, namely, on general logical and semantic grounds. More specifically, on Wallace's understanding, it purported to show that "the extension of standard semantic values to tensed propositions" (143) implies fatalism. Wallace, in his essay, contested this claim: "We can allow contingent future-tensed propositions to take standard truth-values without doing violence to our belief that parts of the universe enjoy at least some degree of causal contingency and that persons enjoy at least some control over what does and will happen to them" (142). The latter belief Wallace holds to be true: "It is not at all the case that [an agent] 'can never do anything he does not do.' . . . This fact seems to me completely and obviously true" (209).

In discussing Wallace's essay I will treat it not as an undergraduate thesis but as a philosophical work in its own right. This attitude is justified not just for the purpose of the present volume; the essay itself calls for this attitude. In fact, the essay offers such a thorough treatment of the questions involved that it sets a new standard for a future defense of Taylor's argument. Or so I will suggest. My goal in this paper is to reconstruct Wallace's critique of Taylor's argument for fatalism in a clear and concise way, so that it is easy to see its main line of reasoning and potential power. In so doing I will be selective in reporting Wallace's views, change the exact order of his discussion, and modify, add to, and simplify some details of his work. My hope is that this will prevent the richness and inventiveness of his essay from overshadowing what I take to be its most pertinent contribution to the debate on Taylor's argument. A secondary goal is to offer clarificatory and critical notes on some of the issues at stake.

The argument Wallace confronts in his essay was presented by Richard Taylor in his 1962 paper, "Fatalism."[2] Taylor's argument is commonly referred to as the *logical* argument for fatalism, or "logical fatalism."[3] Taylor formulates this argument as an argument by example, based on six general presuppositions. The example goes back at least to Aristotle, and it concerns "me"—"a naval commander, about to issue my order of the day to the fleet" (Taylor 1962, 46). The objective situation is that the occurrence or nonoccurrence of a sea battle tomorrow depends entirely on my order. If I issue an order to go to battle, there will be a battle tomorrow; if I issue another order, there will be no sea battle.

Consider the following abbreviations:

O: I issue an order to go to battle,
O': I issue an order to do something other than go to battle,
B: A naval battle occurs tomorrow,
P: It is within my power to do O,
P': It is within my power to do O'.[4]

Using these abbreviations, nonfatalism, or the free-choice position, is expressed by:

P & P';

fatalism is expressed by:

~P ∨ ~P'.

Taylor's argument for fatalism is:[5]

1. $B \supset \sim P'$
2. $\sim B \supset \sim P$
3. $B \vee \sim B$

---

4. $\sim P \vee \sim P'$

This argument is clearly logically valid.[6] This means that to the extent that its premises are all true, its conclusion is guaranteed to be true as well. Taylor informally describes the rationale for his premises as follows:

> Premise 1: "In case [B] is true, then there is, or will be, lacking a condition essential for my doing O', the condition, namely, of there being no naval battle tomorrow."
> Premise 2: "similar reason" (46–47).[7]
> Premise 3: Law of excluded middle.[8]

Taylor claims that these premises (together with their informal rationale) rest on six presuppositions which are held "almost universally in contemporary philosophy" (42) and that if one accepts these presuppositions then one is committed to the argument's conclusion, namely, fatalism. That is, Taylor's claim is that fatalism follows from six widely held and uncontroversial beliefs. These beliefs—his argument's alleged presuppositions—are:[9]

P1. Law of excluded middle.
P2. If S is nonlogically sufficient for S', then S' is necessary for S (S cannot occur without S' also occurring).[10]
P3. If S is necessary for S' (S' cannot occur without S also occurring), then S' is sufficient for S.
P4. S is sufficient for S' if S' is necessary for S.

P5. If S is necessary for A and ~S holds,[11] then no agent can perform A.

P6. Time is not by itself "efficacious."[12]

Taylor describes the gist of his fatalism argument (as based on the above presuppositions) as follows: "What sort of order I issue depends, among other things, on whether a naval battle takes place tomorrow—for in this situation a naval battle tomorrow is (by [P4]) a necessary condition of my doing O, whereas no naval battle tomorrow is equally essential for my doing O'" (47). Assuming the law of excluded middle, he continues, the conclusion follows.

As noted above, Taylor's argument is commonly considered a "logical" argument for fatalism. But is it a purely logical argument? It is clear that if the argument is based (in a nonempty way) on all of P1–P6, it is not purely logical. And in any case, it is clear that if the argument is sound—i.e., both valid and has only true premises (hence *establishes* the truth of its conclusion)—then it is not purely logical, since the truth of premises 1 and 2, assuming they are true, is not attributable to pure logic. Hence to call the position advanced by the argument "logical fatalism" is inaccurate. At the same time, Taylor does not regard the argument as a metaphysical argument either. For example, he insists that the argument does not rest on specific considerations of either time relations or causation (47–48). Wallace, therefore, rightly understands Taylor's argument as (or as intended to be) a "semantic," or a logico-semantic, argument rather than either a logical or a metaphysical argument.

Wallace's most general claim is that a logico-semantic argument cannot establish a metaphysical thesis, in this specific case, fatalism. This claim is both the starting and the ending point of his critique of Taylor. He begins his discussion by saying: "Taylor's central claim . . . is that just a few basic logical and semantic pre-suppositions . . . lead directly to the *metaphysical* conclusion that human beings, agents, have no control over what is going to happen" (Wallace 1985, 144). This claim gives rise to "the Taylor problem" (144), the problem that "a semantic argument . . . appears to force upon us a strange and unhappy metaphysical doctrine that does violence to some of our most basic intuitions about human freedom" (146).

Critically, Wallace asks: "How licit is an argument from linguistic, semantic, and logical premises to a thoroughly metaphysical conclusion?" (150). It is "precisely this move from semantics to metaphysics" that Wallace sets out "to attack in this essay" (150). And having (purportedly) accomplished this task, he concludes his essay by saying: "If Taylor and the fatalists want to force upon us a metaphysical conclusion, they must do metaphysics, *not* semantics. And this seems entirely appropriate" (213).

Wallace's general claim is, then, that a substantive metaphysical thesis like fatalism cannot be established by a logical or a (general) semantic argument; rather, a bona fide metaphysical argument is needed to establish such a thesis. Implicit in this claim is the still stronger and more general claim that metaphysical theses can never be established by purely logical or general semantic principles.

In my view this claim is strictly speaking incorrect, though there is a significant kernel of truth in it. The claim is strictly incorrect because it is always possible to refute a thesis belonging to any science by showing that it contains a logical or a semantic contradiction. Assuming the thesis is metaphysical,[13] this establishes the truth of its negation. But the negation of a metaphysical thesis is itself a metaphysical thesis. Therefore it is in principle possible to establish a metaphysical thesis based on purely logical and/or general semantic principles. At the same time it seems clear that logical and semantic considerations cannot take the place of properly metaphysical considerations in developing our metaphysical theories. After all, logic and general semantics are blind to most (if not all) aspects of reality that are relevant to metaphysics, and as such cannot enlighten us about these aspects.

This blindness to most facets of reality is both the source of logic's and semantics' considerable theoretical efficacy and the source of their theoretical limitations. In logic's case, this has to do with what I elsewhere call its especially strong "degree of invariance" (see, e.g., Sher 2013).[14] The basic idea is this: Logical notions (terms, constants) distinguish only formal features of objects (properties, situations) in the world—features like complementation, intersection, identity, nonemptiness, etc.[15] Since these features are pertinent to all fields of knowledge, logic is efficacious in all fields. In particular, the logical laws apply in all fields. But logic is blind to all nonformal features of the world, including, in our case, its (nonformal) metaphysical features; therefore it is incapable of accounting for these features, and the burden of accounting for these features largely falls on other disciplines. It follows that Wallace's observation that logic has a very limited role in establishing metaphysical theses is, for the most part, warranted. The same applies to general semantics.

Wallace's criticism of Taylor, however, is not limited to his general claim concerning the inability of logic and semantics to yield metaphysical results. He sets out to examine Taylor's argument in detail, and in order to decide how best to critique it he begins by reflecting on the appropriate methodology for accomplishing this task. Having gone over the early literature on this argument[16] and having familiarized himself with a relatively broad range of background literature,[17] he concludes that Taylor was right in claiming that one cannot undermine his argument simply by saying that its conclusion appears absurd. A better methodology, Wallace points out, would be to assign a charitable interpretation to Taylor's argument and show that even under such an interpretation the argument's conclusion—fatalism—does not in fact follow from its premises (assuming they are true). Showing this would demonstrate that Taylor's logico-semantic argument does not establish fatalism or at least would shift the burden of justification to the argument's defenders. In Wallace's words:

> Taylor's thesis is that a certain argument "forces" a fatalistic conclusion upon us. It's clear that I cannot simply reject the conclusion out of hand, but it's just as clear that neither need I accept it and then show somehow by, say, reductio that it is inconsistent in some way. To "refute" Taylor I think I need show only that his conclusion is not *forced* upon us by his argument—for this is his *central* claim. . . . I need to show only that the four-step argument out of Taylor's six presuppositions does not actually yield what Taylor thinks it yields, that his argument is *invalid*. If intuitive rejections of premises and conclusion can be replaced by charitable interpretation, at least semi-rigorous argument, and a demonstration that fatalism follows not even from the most generous way of understanding Taylor's reasoning, the Taylor problem can actually be "solved," or at the very least the burden of argument and proof can be shifted from the opponent of fatalism to its proponent.

> (WALLACE 1985, 159)

These methodological considerations appear to me by and large sound. Nevertheless, one qualification is called for: There is no guarantee that a given charitable interpretation of an argument captures its creator's intentions or that it is the "best" interpretation of this argument. More specifically, there is no guarantee that there is no other compelling interpretation of this argument that does render it sound, i.e., "compels its conclusion on us." But while this qualification puts into question Wallace's claim that he has actually refuted Taylor's claim, it does not affect his claim that the burden of justification has shifted (at least for the time being) to those who wish to defend Taylor. If Wallace's construal of Taylor's argument is indeed reasonable and charitable; if Taylor's argument, under this interpretation, does not establish fatalism; and if Wallace's treatment of the issues arising from Taylor's argument is thorough and compelling, then he can succeed in shifting the burden of justification from Taylor's critics to his allies. Following this methodological strategy, Wallace reasons as follows: "If Taylor's fatalistic argument uses apparently non-controversial premises and appears internally valid, yet results in an obviously defective conclusion, it seems reasonable to suspect that the fatalist engages in some equivocation of his premises, or else some equivocation in the move from what is posited to what is concluded" (159–160).

Naturally, Wallace looks for equivocations and ambiguities in those parts of Taylor's argument/presuppositions that involve, either explicitly or implicitly, potentially problematic elements, like modal, temporal, and causal parameters. Such parameters implicitly appear in steps 1–2 and 4 of Taylor's argument and in presuppositions P2–P5, as was noted by Taylor's early commentators. To see this, consider Taylor's second premise, his second presupposition, and his conclusion. This premise

$$\sim B \supset \sim P$$

says that if no naval battle occurs tomorrow ($\sim B$), then it is not within my power to issue an order to go to battle ($\sim P$).

Now, since its consequent ($\sim P$) says, in effect,

It is not within my power to do O,

it is quite clear that it involves a *modal* operator of some kind. So we may charitably restate premise 2, following Abelson (1963), as

$$\sim B \supset \sim \Diamond O,$$

i.e., as

> If no naval battle occurs tomorrow (~B), then it is impossible that I issue an order to go to battle (~$\Diamond$O).

Furthermore, it is possible to interpret premise 2 charitably as containing *time* markers (B being essentially later than O), as it was by one of Taylor's major defenders, Steven Cahn (1964), whose proposed version of Taylor's argument was "approved" by Taylor. In Cahn's version, the approximate correlate of premise 2 is:

> If it is false at T_2 that a naval battle occurs at T_2, then a necessary condition is lacking for [my] having issued order O at T_1 [so that it is impossible that O occurs at T_1] (Cahn 1964, 103 [8]).

Moreover, Cahn presents his correlate of premise 2 as partly derived from an earlier premise,

> [My] issuing order O at T_1 is a sufficient condition for a naval battle occurring at T_2 (103 [2]),

which not only involves time markers but also suggests that, contrary to Taylor's claim, *causal* considerations are also pertinent to the soundness of his argument. (The relation between O occurring at T_1 and B occurring at T_2 is clearly causal.)

Taylor's second presupposition says that

> If S is nonlogically sufficient for S', then S' is necessary for S.

Clearly, there is a modal operator in this presupposition, and, furthermore, this modal operator is, as Taylor explicitly says, *nonlogical*. But if this modal operator is not logical, then it is not unreasonable to presume that it is physical. And indeed, most of the commentators (Aune 1962, Abelson 1963, Cahn 1964, Saunders 1965, Brown 1965) view Taylor's modalities as physical (empirical, causal) in nature.

Wallace goes a step further.[18] He distinguishes between two types of physical modalities:

(a) Modalities based on compatibility of a given situation with general physical laws (general laws of nature),

(b) Modalities based on compatibility between/among particular situations (assuming both/all are compatible with the general laws of nature).[19]

Wallace (1985, 149) explains the difference between the two types of physical modality by the following examples:

(a)-impossibility: "It is not possible [that I am] both a human being and a quartz crystal"; "it is not possible [that I] travel faster than the speed of light"

(b)-impossibility: "It is not possible [that I], now in Champaign, Illinois, [will touch] a building in Massachusetts thirty seconds from now"

The impossibilities involved in Taylor's argument (having to do with giving an order one day and there being or not being a sea battle the next day), Wallace points out, do not seem to be (a)-impossibilities. They are more likely to be (b)-impossibilities and as such might in principle involve times and/or causal relations.

Turning to the conclusion of Taylor's argument,

$\sim P \lor \sim P'$,

it is clear, given our discussion above, that it, too, involves modal operators and as such is naturally expressed by

$\sim\lozenge O \lor \sim\lozenge O'$

or, based on the observation that the modality in question is not logical, and using "θ" to express the appropriate type of possibility,

$\sim\theta O \lor \sim\theta O'$.

Now, implicit nonlogical modalities, causal relations, and time indices—all these provide a fertile ground for ambiguities and equivocations, and this suggests that Wallace's strategy of looking for these in Taylor's argument is a reasonable strategy (if not one that is guaranteed to succeed).

But is it really a reasonable strategy? One might object that Taylor's argument is *logically* valid, and logically valid arguments have the property of monotonicity, meaning that by adding information—including information on the modal, temporal, and causal parameters implicit in their premises and conclusions—one cannot undermine their validity. So Wallace cannot undermine Taylor's argument by adding new modal, temporal, and/or causal information to its premises.

This objection, however, does not pose an insurmountable obstacle for Wallace. He may claim that while Taylor's argument, as originally formulated, is logically valid, its conclusion, as originally formulated, is *not tantamount to fatalism.* Taylor's original conclusion is ambiguous: depending how one construes its implicit modal and temporal operators, it is either a fatalistic conclusion or a nonfatalistic conclusion. So, one challenge open to Wallace is a challenge to Taylor's claim that his argument establishes *fatalism.* And this, indeed, is what Wallace does.

What, then, are the two ways in which Wallace disambiguates Taylor's conclusion? Wallace distinguishes between a genuinely fatalist conclusion, Conclusion 1, and a nonfatalist conclusion, Conclusion 2, which are both compatible with Taylor's original conclusion:

~P ∨ ~P′

Using "t_0" to indicate the present day before I issue my order, "t_1" to indicate the present day when I issue my order, and "t_2" to indicate the following day, tomorrow, the day in which the order I issue will either cause a sea battle to occur or result in no sea battle occurring (say, at the end of the day), Wallace formulates Conclusions 1 and 2 in a way that could be construed as follows:

Conclusion 1: At-t_0: [~◇ (at-t_1:O) ∨ ~◇ (at-t_1:O′)]
Conclusion 2: At-t_2: [~◇ (at-t_1:O) ∨ ~◇ (at-t_1:O′)]

The wide-scope occurrence of the time indices indicates what Wallace calls the "context of evaluation", i.e., the context of evaluating the truth (correctness) of the ensuing statements, or the context of the "situations-at-times . . . bear[ing] on [the] modality [or modalities in its scope]" (189). The narrow-scope occurrences of the time indices indicate the "context of occurrence"—the time period in which the situation in the scope of the modal operators (or a situation not in the scope of any modal operator) is said to occur.

What is the difference between the two conclusions with respect to fatalism? Conclusion 1 says that today the future is not open for me: either I cannot issue order O or I cannot issue order O′. Conclusion 2 says that looking back tomorrow at what transpired today, it will become clear that certain things could not have occurred today. Or: what transpires tomorrow rules out either the possibility that the day before I in fact issued an order to go to battle or the possibility that the day before I in fact issued a no-battle order. Now, Wallace observes, of the two, only Conclusion 1 correctly expresses the idea of fatalism. Fatalism says that today (at t_0) it is not open to me, for one reason or another, a reason situated in the past or present (at t_0 or earlier), rather than in the future (t_2), to choose what order to give and act on this choice. It does not say that what actually transpires tomorrow is incompatible with some situation having transpired today.

Wallace clarifies this point by a pair of examples (173), analogous to Conclusions 1 and 2:

> Example 1 (analog of Conclusion 1): "It couldn't rain last night; last night a high-pressure ridge was keeping all rain-clouds away."
>
> Example 2 (analog of Conclusion 2): "It can't have rained last night; there are no puddles on the sidewalk this morning."

And Wallace concludes: Conclusion 2, unlike Conclusion 1, does not express a fatalism thesis. "The absence of a battle [tomorrow has no bearing on my] freedom and power to give order O [today] if [I choose]" (175).

Now, this line of reasoning seems reasonable (if not indefeasible), and if it is, then Wallace's next task is to show us that Taylor's argument does not entail Conclusion 1.

Informally, we can describe the line of reasoning used by Wallace in performing this task as follows: Suppose Taylor's sea-battle scenario does imply Conclusion 1. Then, the things that prevent me from issuing either order O or order O′ are either laws of nature or causal circumstances. Since no law of nature prevents me from issuing either order, it is causal circumstances that would prevent me from doing so. But causality is unidirectional, proceeding from past to future and not from future to past (or, at least, that is what most philosophers believe, which is the crucial point for Taylor). Therefore it would be causal circumstances holding *prior to* my issuing my order that would prevent me from performing O/O′ at t_1. However, Taylor's sea-battle scenario does not involve any such circumstances. Therefore, Taylor's argument is compatible with the negation of Conclusion 1; i.e., his argument *does not entail* Conclusion 1.

In setting out to show this more rigorously, we note that as originally formulated, the premises of Taylor's argument do not imply either Conclusion 1 or Conclusion 2. This is because they are not formulated in the same language as those conclusions. To see whether Taylor's premises imply either conclusion, then, we need to rewrite them in the language of these conclusions. The resulting argument, with the two alternative consequences, would be something like:

1′. At-t_2: [(at-t_2:B) ⊃ (~◇ (at-t_1:O′)]
2′. At-t_2: [(at-t_2:~B) ⊃ (~◇ (at-t_1:O)]
3′. At-all-t: [(at-t:B) ∨ (at-t:~B)]

4′-1. At-t_0: [~◇ (at-t_1:O) ∨ ~◇ (at-t_1:O′)]
4′-2. At-t_2: [~◇ (at-t_1:O) ∨ ~◇ (at-t_1:O′)],

where "B" now abbreviates "A sea battle occurs."

Now, Wallace claims that the argument <1′, 2′, 3′, 4′-1> is invalid, and to establish this claim he delineates a model, call it "M," in which premises 1′, 2′, and 3′ are all true, and 4′-1 is false. Simplifying, we can construe his model as follows: There are two different worlds—W and W′, three time indices—t_0, t_1, and t_2—and a binary relation of physical compatibility between worlds-at-times (a special type of accessibility relation between worlds).

Time t_0
World W: No pertinent information. (This means: No causal obstacles to anything concerning O, O', and B at later times.)
World W': Same as W.
Time t_1
World W: O occurs.
World W': O' occurs.
Time t_2
World W: B occurs.
World W': ~B occurs.

Compatibility Relations Between Worlds-at-Times:

(i) W at-t_0 is compatible with W at-t_1, W' at-t_1, W at-t_2, and W' at-t_2.
(ii) W' at-t_0 is compatible with W at-t_1, W' at-t_1, W at-t_2, and W' at-t_2.
(iii) W at-t_2 is compatible with W at-t_1 and incompatible with W' at-t_1.
(iv) W' at-t_2 is compatible with W' at-t_1 and incompatible with W at-t_1.

Now, assuming (as the majority of philosophers presumably do) that the law of excluded middle holds in all possible worlds at all times, it is clear that 1', 2', 3', and 4'–2 are all true in M, while 4'–1 is false. That is, when formulated as above, Taylor's premises do not *force* fatalism upon us.

What are we to make of this result? It seems to me that what Wallace has shown is sufficient to support at least part of his claim, namely, that on his charitable construal of Taylor's argument (charitable in rendering its three premises true in an intuitively judicious way), this argument does not "force" fatalism upon us. Taylor's argument might entail Conclusion 2, but Conclusion 2 is not tantamount to fatalism. The question whether Taylor's "proof" of fatalism fails, period, depends on whether, on closer examination, Wallace's construal of his argument is optimal, and this I leave as an open question. But given Wallace's sensible challenge to Taylor, his countermodel, and his thought-out discussion of the issues involved, I think it is reasonable to conclude that Wallace succeeded in shifting the burden of justification to Taylor's supporters. Taylor's supporters have either to show that his argument's original conclusion is, as it stands, a genuine fatalism conclusion or else to reconstruct his argument so it leads to a genuine fatalism conclusion. But neither is easy to do. For example, to defend Taylor's claim under a reconstrual of his argument requires showing that either the argument has no countermodels or that its conclusion is derivable from its premises in a(n appropriate) system in which all the premises are true. And both are difficult to accomplish. Negative-existential claims are often notoriously difficult to establish, and the construction of a well-motivated proof system that would validate (a reconstructed version of) Taylor's argument is not an easy task either.[20]

Taylor might, however, raise several objections to Wallace's criticism that we have not considered yet. One of these is an objection he did raise with respect to other critics, namely, that since essentially *the same* argument as his argument for fatalism about the *future* succeeds in entailing fatalism about the *past*, which is something the majority of philosophers accept, it is problematic to argue that the argument fails in the former case. In Taylor's words:

> We all are . . . fatalists with respect to the past. No one considers past events as being within his power to control.
>
> (TAYLOR 1962, 45)

> Not one of my critics has seen . . . that the very refutations they give of my fatalism about the future would work just as well to prove that we should not be fatalists about the past.
>
> (TAYLOR 1963B, 87)

> No one feels the slightest suspicion about the . . . argument [for fatalism about the past]. Indeed, the logic of it seems so obvious that one might well wonder what can be the point of spelling it all out so exactly. But that is because everyone is already a fatalist about the past—no one supposes it is up to him what has happened, or that past things are still within his power.
>
> The thing to note, however, is that these two arguments are formally identical, except only for tenses.
>
> (TAYLOR 1963A, 62)

The argument Taylor refers to is an argument he himself gave, an argument that, like his argument for fatalism about the future, relates to a specific scenario and, according to Taylor, is based on the same six presuppositions as the latter. Here the "actions" in question are (i) S—seeing a headline announcing a sea battle yesterday when I open my morning newspaper, and (ii) S′—seeing an incompatible headline when I open the paper this morning. It is assumed that the headline I see accurately describes what has transpired yesterday. Using the following abbreviations,

S: When I open the newspaper I see the headline announcing a sea battle yesterday,

S′: When I open the newspaper I see the headline announcing something other than a sea
battle yesterday,

B: A naval battle occurs yesterday,

P: It is in my power to do S,

P′: It is in my power to do S′.

Taylor's argument for fatalism about the past is then exactly the same as his argument for fatalism about the future (though with a somewhat different symbolization key):

1. $B \supset {\sim}P'$
2. ${\sim}B \supset {\sim}P$
3. $B \vee {\sim}B$
4. ${\sim}P \vee {\sim}P'$.

(BASED ON TAYLOR 1962, 45)

But this is not sufficient to defend the soundness of Taylor's argument for fatalism about the *future*. First, acknowledging the truth of fatalism about the past does not mean accepting any argument whatsoever for such fatalism. It is in principle possible that fatalism about the past is justified but that Taylor's argument for it is not sound (i.e., it is either invalid or at least one of its premises is false). Second, it is in principle possible that the conclusion of Taylor's argument for "fatalism about the past" is not really tantamount to fatalism about the past or is ambiguous between fatalism about the past and another thesis. If this is the case, it is possible that his argument is a sound argument for the second thesis but not for fatalism about the past. Third, it is possible that in spite of the external similarity between Taylor's arguments for fatalism about the past and the future, there are significant differences between these two arguments (reflected in the difference between their symbolization keys and the situations the two arguments relate to). Taylor himself acknowledges a difference in tense, or time indices, between the two arguments. If Wallace and others are right, and causality plays a central (if implicit) role in Taylor's arguments, then given the unidirectionality of causation, differences in time indices might be significant. Fourth, it might be questioned whether the two actions in Taylor's scenario are of a kind that can be used to adjudicate questions of free will, whether seeing a particular headline when one opens the paper can be considered a freely chosen action at all, either past looking or future looking (comparable to giving an order). Finally, it is possible that on Wallace's reconstruction of the two arguments, the argument for fatalism with respect to the past is sound while the argument for fatalism with respect to the future is not.

Wallace himself claims that the last possibility is the case; namely, Taylor's argument for past-fatalism, unlike his argument for future-fatalism, is valid and sound. But to evaluate his claim that Taylor's argument for past-fatalism is sound, it is not sufficient to construct a single model that agrees with it. To establish validity claims we have to show that the argument has no counter-models, and this requires constructing a general system in which all the relevant models are determined. Wallace does construct such a system, a system he calls "J," but attempting to evaluate this system (which, among other things, is only partially delineated) would lead us away from the issues we are focusing on in this paper.[21] Regardless of Wallace's validity claim, however, it appears that defending Taylor's argument for future-fatalism based on its similarity to his argument for past-fatalism is potentially problematic on several counts.

Taylor might try to defend his claim on future-fatalism on different grounds. For example, he might criticize Wallace's critique on the ground that it is committed to viewing truth as *relative* while truth is in fact *absolute*. In particular, Taylor might argue, relativity to a *context of evaluation* makes no sense.

Today, however, there is an influential response to this objection, thanks to John MacFarlane (2003, 2005, 2011). MacFarlane is aware of the widespread antipathy to truth relativism among contemporary philosophers: "Analytic philosophers tend to regard relativism about truth as hopelessly confused, easily refuted, and even a sign of deficient intellectual character" (2005, 321). They have a "deeply entrenched theoretical commitment to the absoluteness of . . . truth" (2003, 327). MacFarlane rejects this commitment both on factual and on conceptual grounds: Factually, "some of the things we say and think *are* . . . sensitive [to context]" (2011, 138, my italics); conceptually, "the possibility of . . . expressions [which are sensitive to context] is coherent and intelligible" (2011, 139). Indeed, MacFarlane points out: "No one would deny that the truth of sentences must be relativized to context [sometimes]: 'I am cold' has no absolute truth-value, but is true in relation to some contexts of utterance, false in relation to others" (2003, 322). And there are other widely accepted types of relativity: "Many relativizations of truth are entirely orthodox. In model theory we talk of sentences being true relative to a model and an assignment of values to the variables, and in formal semantics we talk of sentences being true relative to a speaker and time, or more generally (following Kaplan 1989) a context of use" (2005, 322).

MacFarlane's own contribution is the introduction of a new type of relativity, which, he argues, is essential for accounting for the truth (falsehood, indeterminacy) of certain sentences and utterances, for example, future contingents. The relativity required for understanding the truth conditions of sentences of this kind, he says, is relativity to "*contexts of assessment*" (2005, 321):

> We must relativize the truth of utterances to a *context of assessment*, and we must relativize the truth of sentences to both a context of utterance and a context of assessment. This amounts to recognizing a new kind of linguistic context-sensitivity: sentence truth can vary not just with features of the context of utterance [and other familiar contexts] but with features of the context of assessment.
>
> (2003, 322)

And he adds: "It is failure to make room for this kind of context sensitivity that has left us with the traditional menu of unsatisfactory solutions to [such problems as] the problem of future contingents"

(2003, 322). "In order to make good sense of future contingents, we must allow the truth of utterances to be relativized to the context from which they are being assessed" (2003, 328).

And what is truth relativity to context(s) of assessment? It is "truth at a *point of evaluation*. . . . Points of evaluation are sequences of parameters, for example, speaker, location of utterance, time and assignment" (2003, 329). Consider the following example:

> "There will be a sea battle tomorrow," says Themistocles, at a time when it is objectively indeterminate whether there will be a sea battle the next day. Is his assertion accurate or inaccurate? The question can only be answered, according to a relativist view, relative to a particular context of assessment. Themistocles' assertion is inaccurate as assessed from the moment at which it is made (m_0), accurate as assessed from a moment one day later on a possible future history with a sea battle (m_1), and inaccurate as assessed from a moment one day later on a possible future history without a sea battle (m_2).
>
> (2011, 133)

But this is quite similar to what Wallace said about statements concerning the possibility that we act in one way or another in the future. MacFarlane, thus, can be viewed as offering a vindication of Wallace's claim that the truth of some statements requires relativity to multiple contexts, specifically, in the case of free will and fatalism, relativity to *time of occurrence* and to *time of evaluation*.

Bringing Wallace to the contemporary scene, we might say that, in a sense, his essay anticipated MacFarlane. Wallace's "context of evaluation" is a forerunner of MacFarlane's "context of assessment," and Wallace's "time of evaluation" is one of the possible parameters in MacFarlane's context of assessment. In this sense, then, Wallace was ahead of his time. This is a good note on which to end our assessment of his honors thesis's contribution to philosophy.[22]

NOTES

1. A more recent characterization of fatalism in the same spirit is: "FATALISM is the thesis that whatever happens must happen; every event or state of affairs that occurs, must occur, while the nonoccurrence of every event and state of affairs is likewise necessitated. With respect to human affairs, fatalism claims that we lack the power (capability, ability) to perform any actions other than the ones that we do, in fact, perform. Our belief that there are alternative courses of action available to our decisions and choices is mistaken. As a result, there is no such thing as (libertarian) free will" (Bernstein 2005, 65).

2. See also Taylor (1963a), chap. 5.

3. See, e.g., Rice (2010).

4. O, O', and B are based, almost verbatim, on Taylor (1962, 46). P and P' are the two conjuncts in Taylor's conclusion. I have changed some of the letters in Taylor's abbreviation key to make their association with the sentences they abbreviate more immediate and have added some abbreviations to make the logic of the argument clearer.

5. This is a somewhat simplified version of Taylor's argument (Taylor 1962, 46–47). A formulation that is more similar to the original would be:

    1. $T(B) \supset \sim P'$
    2. $T(\sim B) \supset \sim P$
    3. $T(B) \lor T(\sim B)$
    4. $\sim P \lor \sim P'$,

    where "T" abbreviates "It is true that." But the simpler formulation is sufficient for our purpose.

6. Assuming classical logic, which is—significantly for Taylor's claim (see below)—the prevalent logic today.

7. These justifications of premises 1 and 2 are potentially open to criticisms, but since this is not essential for understanding Wallace's critique, I will not discuss it further here.

8. Or, for the alternative formulation of the argument, the principle of bivalence. (In the original Taylor text, however, only the law of excluded middle is mentioned.)

9. Based on Taylor (1962, 43–44).

10. S and S' are arbitrary states of affairs or conditions. P2–P5 are construed as universal (i.e., they hold for any S, S', and A [A is an arbitrary act]).

Informally, S is *nonlogically sufficient* for S' iff (if and only if) S ensures S' but does not logically entail S'. My formulations of P2 and P3 are affected by Taylor's claim that P4 *follows logically* from P2 and P3.

11. I.e., S does not occur "at the same or any other time." (Taylor 1962, 43).

12. Taylor explains: "the mere passage of time does not augment or diminish the capacities of anything and, in particular, . . . it does not enhance or decrease an agent's powers or abilities." (1962, 44).

13. Something that might be reflected in the thesis having nonlogical vocabulary in addition to logical vocabulary, it being task of metaphysics to restore consistency to its theories in light of the discovery of a contradiction, etc.

14. Intuitively, the relation between invariance and blindness is that a notion is invariant under all (actual and potential) variations or changes in the world that it is blind to.

15. Which are the objectual correlates of the logical constants.

16. Aune (1962), Abelson (1963), Taylor (1963a, 1964), Cahn (1964), Saunders (1965), Brown (1965), and possibly others.

17. Which includes Ayer (1963), Kripke (1963), Lehrer and Taylor (1964), Lewis (1973), von Wright (1974), Haack (1974), MacArthur (1976), White (1977, 1979), Loux (1979), Dowty, Wall, and Peters (1981), Landman (1984), and possibly others.

18. The following is based on Wallace (1985, 149, 165).

19. He calls these "situational" physical modalities, but we will not use this term here.

20. Whether Wallace's criticism applies to Cahn's reconstruction of Taylor's argument I will leave an open question.

21. For the same reason I have not examined Wallace's claim that Taylor's argument for future-fatalism establishes Conclusion 2.

22. I would like to thank two anonymous referees for their comments.

REFERENCES

Abelson, R. 1963. "Taylor's Fatal Fallacy." *Philosophical Review* 72, no. 1. Reprinted in Cahn and Eckert 2011, 79–83. Citations refer to the reprint.

Aune, B. 1962. "Fatalism and Professor Taylor." *Philosophical Review* 71, no. 4. Reprinted in Cahn and Eckert 2011, 69–78. Citations refer to the reprint.

Ayer, A. J. 1936. *The Concept of a Person and Other Essays.* London: Macmillan.

Bernstein, M. 2005. "Fatalism." In *The Oxford Handbook of Free Will*, ed. R. Kane. Oxford: Oxford University Press.

Brown, C. D. 1965. "Fallacies in Taylor's 'Fatalism.'" *Journal of Philosophy* 62, no. 13. Reprinted in Cahn and Eckert 2011, 127–132. Citations refer to the reprint.

Cahn, S. M. 1964. "Fatalistic Arguments." *Journal of Philosophy* 61, no. 10. Reprinted in Cahn and Eckert 2011: 93–106. Citations refer to the reprint.

Cahn, S., and M. Eckert, eds. 2011. *Fate, Time, and Language: An Essay on Free Will*, by David Foster Wallace. New York: Columbia University Press.

Dowty, D. R., R. E. Wall, and S. Peters. 1981. *Introduction to Montague Semantics*. Dordrecht: Kluwer.

Haack, S. 1974. *Deviant Logic*. Cambridge: Cambridge University Press.

Kaplan, D. 1989. "Demonstratives: An Essay on the Semantics, Logic, Metaphysics, and Epistemology of Demonstratives and Other Indexicals." In *Themes from Kaplan*, ed. J. Almog, J. Perry, and H. Wettstein. Oxford: Oxford University Press.

Kripke, S. 1963. "Semantical Considerations on Modal Logic." *Acta Philosophica Fennica* 16: 83–94.

Landman, F. 1984. "Data Semantics for Attitude Reports." *Logique et Analyse* 106: 165–192.

Lehrer, K., and R. Taylor. 1964. "Time, Truth and Modalities." *Mind* 74: 890–898.

Lewis, D. 1973. "Causation." *Journal of Philosophy* 70: 556–567.

Loux, R., ed. 1979. *The Possible and the Actual*. Ithaca, N.Y.: Cornell University Press.

MacFarlane, J. 2003. "Future Contingents and Relative Truth." *Philosophical Quarterly* 53: 321–336.

——. 2005. "Making Sense of Relative Truth." *Proceedings of the Aristotelian Society* 105: 321–339.

——. 2011. "Relativism." In *The Routledge Companion to the Philosophy of Language*. ed., D. Graff Fara and G. Russell. New York: Routledge.

Prior, A. 1967. *Past, Present, and Future*. Oxford: Clarendon.

Rice, H. 2010. "Fatalism." In *Stanford Encyclopedia of Philosophy*, ed. E. M. Zalta. http://plato.stanford.edu/entries/fatalism/.

Saunders, J. T. 1965. "Fatalism and Ordinary Language." *Journal of Philosophy* 62, no. 8. Reprinted in Cahn and Eckert 2011, 111–125. Citations refer to the reprint.

Sher, G. 2013. "The Foundational Problem of Logic." *Bulletin of Symbolic Logic* 19: 145–198.

Taylor, R. 1962. "Fatalism." *Philosophical Review* 71, no. 1. Reprinted in Cahn and Eckert 2011, 41–51. Citations refer to the reprint.

———. 1963a. *Metaphysics.* Englewood Cliffs, N.J.: Prentice Hall.

———. 1963b. "A Note on Fatalism." *Philosophical Review* 72, no. 4. Reprinted in Cahn and Eckert 2011, 85–88. Citations refer to the reprint.

———. 1964. Comment. *Journal of Philosophy* 61, no. 10. Reprinted in Cahn and Eckert 2011, 107–110. Citations refer to the reprint.

Von Wright, G. H. 1974. *Causality and Determinism.* New York: Columbia University Press.

Wallace, D. F. 1985. "Richard Taylor's 'Fatalism' and the Semantics of Physical Modality." Honors Thesis, Amherst College. In Cahn and Eckert 2011, 141–216.

———. 2005. "Kenyon College Commencement Address." http://moreintelligentlife .com/story/david-foster-wallace-in-his-own-words.

White, A. R. 1977. *Modal Thinking.* Ithaca, N.Y.: Cornell University Press.

3

FATALISM AND THE METAPHYSICS OF CONTINGENCY

M. ORESTE FIOCCO

CONTINGENCY AND THE SPECTER OF FATALISM

Contingency is the presence of nonactualized possibility in the world. Given contingency, the world as it *actually* is is incomplete not in that there *are* features of reality beyond those that actually exist but in that there *could be*. If there is contingency, a systematic metaphysics need provide some account of this possibility, including its source and relations to other features of the world. However, *fatalism* is a view of reality on which there is no contingency. On this view, the world as it actually is is entirely complete: every detail must be just as it is, and there neither is, nor could be, anything beyond this. Hence, there is no need to account for the possibility in the world, for there is none.

It is contingency that permits *agency*, for if nothing were possible beyond what is actual, *every* feature of reality would be brute, in that it would *have to be* just as it is. There would be no distinction, then, between mere happening and intentional behavior. An action, the result of intentional behavior, seems to require—at the very least—being amenable to a certain sort of explanation, one in terms of the mental states of a conscious being. Yet any such explanation is void if every feature of the world simply must be as it is. Hence, in a world in which there is no contingency, there is no place for the direction of an agent or for agency itself. Fatalism is inimical to a natural view of oneself as an active being capable of responding to and freely contributing, even if only slightly, to what the world is like.

In light of this, there has traditionally been much interest in contingency. Such interest has long been embarrassed by the contention that simple and plausible assumptions about the world lead to fatalism. At the outset of Western metaphysical thought, Aristotle presented reasons for thinking that contingency requires the world in time to be a certain way and that this limits what is true of the world. I largely concur with Aristotle—most, however, do not. It is worth examining the Aristotelian considerations in a contemporary context, for what emerges are two incompatible accounts of contingency, two very different ways of situating possibility in the world.

I begin with the Aristotelian argument in the modern form in which it is presented in Richard Taylor's ruminations on fatalism. Appreciation of this argument has been stultified by a question pertaining to the source of necessity and possibility and a closely related one regarding the nature of metaphysics itself; this can be seen via the criticism of Taylor by his contemporaries. With these questions addressed, the heart of the matter—necessity and possibility in a temporal world—comes to light. This issue is investigated through an important later criticism of Taylor by David Foster Wallace. Wallace's critique is significant because it brings to the fore the crucial notion for understanding contingency in a temporal world, that of *synchronic possibility*, the idea that incompatible states of affairs are possible at a single moment. This notion provides the basis of distinguishing two systematic accounts of truth, modality and time: two metaphysics of contingency. On one account, Taylor's Aristotelian argument is straightforwardly valid and compelling; on the other, it is fallacious. In closing, I present reasons why the former account, supporting the Aristotelian views of time and truth, is correct and make some comments to ameliorate this conclusion.

FATALISM AND TAYLOR'S ARGUMENT

Aristotle's (1987, 17–19) argument that contingency entails perhaps surprising views of the world in time and of truth is compressed and, largely for this reason, cryptic. Richard Taylor's modern presentation of essentially the same argument is more elaborate.

Taylor's Premises

Taylor contends that "presuppositions made almost universally in contemporary philosophy yield a proof that fatalism is true" (Taylor 1962a, 42). This proof rests on six premises. Three of these are merely definitional. Nevertheless, they are controversial, for they introduce the modal notions employed in Taylor's discussion, and these are vexed (as discussed in "Metaphysics and the Source of Necessity and Possibility," below).

The first of these definitional premises is that if something, some state of affairs or condition or feature of the world, in itself guarantees the existence of another, then the first is *sufficient* for the second, that is, it *must* be the case that if the former exists, so does the latter. Similarly, and this is Taylor's second premise, if some state of affairs, S_1, requires the existence of another, S_2, that is, if it is *impossible* that S_1 exist without S_2, then S_2 is *necessary* for S_1. The third premise follows from these two: if some state of affairs, S_1, is sufficient for another, S_2, then S_2 is necessary for S_1.

With these premises, Taylor takes himself to be explicating the standard notions of a *necessary* and a *sufficient condition*. Yet he seems to recognize that his application of the notions is somewhat atypical, so he provides further comments to illuminate the relations based on them. He states their relata need not exist at the same moment and that the relations are not "logical," that is, conceptual, so they can hold between things in the world and not merely one's ideas or representations of such things.[1] Moreover,

Taylor makes clear that the relations are neither physical nor nomological and, in particular, have nothing to do with causation. Thus, for example, one state of affairs being a sufficient condition for another is no indication that the former is a cause of the latter or connected to it by any law of nature. Taylor is explicit that his argument makes no recourse to physics (1962a, 42) and that his conclusions with respect to contingency are made "without any reference to causation" (48).

The other premises of Taylor's argument are more obviously substantial, pertaining to truth, the necessary connections between things in the world, and the nature of the world in time. The first is an assumption of bivalence: *every proposition whatsoever is either true or, if not true, false.* The second is presented as the claim that no agent can do something if some necessary condition for that action is lacking. Although this makes clear the relevance of Taylor's discussion to concerns about agency, the point can be generalized to draw out its deeper metaphysical consequences: *no state of affairs or condition or feature of the world can occur if some necessary condition for that state of affairs does not exist.*

The premise about temporal reality is the least perspicuous. As Taylor states it, it is that "time is not by itself 'efficacious,'" (1962a, 44) and immediately explains that by this he means that "the mere passage of time" (44) does not affect the capacities of a thing. So if a thing loses some capacity, this is because it has undergone some change in its nature and not merely because the moment at which it exists has gone, for instance, from future to present or present to past. The crux of the premise is, then, that *when a thing exists does not by itself affect the nature of that thing.* Thus, Taylor seems to be assuming a familiar view of the nature of temporal reality, one on which it is *ontologically homogeneous,* that is, the view that there are many moments of time and that all these moments, and the things existing at them, are equally real.[2] This interpretation of Taylor's premise is corroborated by comments he makes later in his discussion,[3] most clearly when he states that fatalism follows not from

> the mere *temporal* relations between . . . states of affairs, but the very existence of those states of affairs themselves; and according to our first presupposition [that every proposition whatsoever is either true or, if not true, false] the fact of tomorrow's containing, or lacking, [some state of affairs], as the case may be, is no less a fact than yesterday's containing or lacking one.
>
> (TAYLOR 1962A, 48)

The Argument

Given these premises, Taylor, alluding to Aristotle, presents a picturesque argument that there is no contingency. He imagines that he is a naval commander and that his order is a sufficient condition for a sea battle tomorrow; likewise, a different order is sufficient for there to be no battle. Stripped of extraneous detail, Taylor's argument is this: a given state of affairs, s (e.g., an order for battle's being given), at an imminent moment, m_1, is a sufficient condition for a distinct state of affairs, n (e.g., a sea battle), at some subsequent moment, m_2. The absence of s at m_1, that is, the existence then of the incompatible state of affairs, $-s$, is a sufficient condition for a distinct state of affairs, $-n$, which is incompatible with n, at m_2. The assumption that at m_1 both s is possible and $-s$ is possible is untenable. This is because it is supposed that the proposition that n occurs at m_2 is true or, if not true, false; if it is false, then the proposition that $-n$ occurs at m_2 is true. Consequently, it is supposed that at m_2 either n occurs or $-n$ does. If n occurs, then $-n$ cannot, in which case $-s$ cannot occur (because $-n$ is a necessary condition of $-s$); on the other hand, if $-n$ occurs, then n cannot, in which case s cannot occur. Thus, either s or $-s$ is impossible at m_1. One of the two occurs at m_1, and whichever actually does, that state of affairs must occur. This contravenes the possibility of a nonactualized state of affairs at m_1. Since there is nothing special about these moments or states of affairs or the relations in which they stand, this argument demonstrates that given Taylor's premises there is no contingency.

Indeed from Taylor's assumption regarding the ontological homogeneity of temporal reality, it is clear that it follows that any state of affairs is related to some other in such a way as to make the above argument applicable: The existence of some state of affairs, s, at some moment is a sufficient condition for the subsequent existence at m_w, say, one week later, of a distinct state of affairs, n, namely, the state of affairs that s occurs one week prior to m_w. The argument, therefore, has purchase on the world, and it is perplexing, for it demonstrates that there is no contingency—something that seems to be an immediate and, hence, indubitable feature of the world—from premises all of which are familiar and not without appeal.

Taylor's Conclusion

Taylor, however, does not accept fatalism. This should be clear from his own response to the foregoing argument or, if not from this, from his body of work.[4] It is odd, then, that he is often thought to be a fatalist (by, for example, Bruce Aune [1962, 69] and Wallace [1985, 143]). Rather, following Aristotle, Taylor concludes that given contingency, one must reject at least one of the premises of the fatalistic argument. So he denies that every proposition whatsoever is either true or, if not true, false. Denying this allows him to reject the claim, crucial to the argument, that the proposition that n occurs at m_2 is true or, if not true, false.

Taylor recognizes that rejecting such claims about the future requires a revision of one's account of temporal reality. If it is not the case that the proposition that n occurs at m_2 is true or, if not true, false, then—assuming that any true proposition is grounded in some feature of reality[5]—it is *not* the case that either n or $-n$ occurs at m_2. It presumably *is* the case, however, that for any state of affairs, either it or its contradictory occurs or has occurred (suspending, for the nonce, any concerns about vagueness). Therefore, with respect to the existence of states of affairs, reality as it is subsequent to this moment has a different status from the way it is (or was); the ontological homogeneity of temporal reality is false, so *when* a thing exists does by itself affect the nature of that thing. Taylor acknowledges that these premises about truth and the world in time are "inseparably linked, standing or falling together" (Taylor 1962a, 51).

I think the rejection of these two related assumptions about truth and temporal reality is, in the end, the appropriate response to Taylor's Aristotelian argument. Most, however, disagree. Many believe Taylor's argument is fallacious and maintain that there is no need to revise the familiar assumptions on which it is based. I think such criticism is mistaken, though not unreasonable. Taylor leaves some key assumptions tacit, and this has misled his critics. These assumptions need to be articulated to appreciate the force of the argument.

METAPHYSICS AND THE SOURCE OF NECESSITY AND POSSIBILITY

Many of those who have been critical of Taylor, especially his contemporaries, have simply misunderstood his project and the basis of his Aristotelian argument. The misunderstanding concerns the *modality*—the source of necessity and possibility— pertinent to the argument and the very conception of metaphysics associated with this modality. Confusion on these grounds has led several philosophers to make criticisms that fail even to engage with the argument.

The Notion of a Modality

A *modality* is a basis of related conditions from which to qualify a claim's truth. Given this basis, a claim *must, could not,* or *could* be true; that is, relative to a modality, the claim has the status of being *necessary, impossible,* or *possible.* More generally, a modality determines certain relations in which things stand; hence, given a particular basis of related conditions, two things are *necessarily connected* (i.e., the one necessitates or entails the other), or *incompatible* (i.e., the one *precludes* the other), or *compatible with* each other.

If there is contingency, there are claims that, despite not representing what actually is the case, could be true; if there is no contingency—if fatalism is true—there are no such claims. The question of what modality is relevant here is of the utmost importance. Examples of different modalities are: the rules of a natural language, the class of concepts by which one identifies things and characterizes the world, the natural laws governing the material world, the laws of logic, the natures of things in themselves, the claims one takes oneself to know. Thus, given the rules of English, the claim that all bachelors are unmarried must be true; given (the current understanding of) the natural laws of interest to physicists, the claim that there is a vehicle that travels faster than light could not be true. Given a traditional account of concepts, the claim that there is water that is not H_2O could be true. Similarly, given the natural laws of interest to physicists, combustion necessitates oxygen; given these laws, combustion is compatible with wood.

Two Understandings of Metaphysics

When Taylor's argument appeared in the early 1960s it was orthodox—absolutely taken for granted—that the only modalities pertinent to philosophy were *linguistic*: those of logic, as codified by different formal languages, and the rules of a natural language, including the concepts associated with these. Of course, the modality of the laws of nature was legitimate, but it was the domain of natural scientists.

This orthodoxy reflects a particular understanding of the world, one deriving from a number of sources, notably Hume and Kant, and the impetus for the so-called linguistic turn of mainstream analytic philosophy through most of the twentieth century. On this understanding, much of the basal structure of reality—what kinds of things exist, the natures of individual things, the relations in which they stand—is a result of the interaction with the world of the minds of conscious beings. In particular, the structure arises from how conscious beings react to a differentiated yet amorphous world, how they think about it and express these thoughts via language. Precisely how much worldly structure arises in this way is a profound and disputatious question; however, what is supposed not to be controversial is that since much of this structure comes from the activity of conscious beings, necessary connections—and, consequently, what is compatible and incompatible—are reflections of the workings of mind. They are relations of ideas or concepts or the expression of such in language: hence, the only legitimate *metaphysical* modalities are linguistic. From this understanding comes a particular conception of metaphysics, one on which its purpose is to make clear the linguistic-cum-conceptual rules by which reality is structured. These rules and their relations, which are supposed to be accessible to any competent thinker or speaker, are to be illuminated by a process of reflection and analysis.

In opposition to this is a quite different understanding of the world, one rooted in Aristotle and decidedly unfashionable in the twentieth century. On this understanding, the basal structure of reality is entirely independent of the minds of conscious beings: there are many kinds and individual instances of these kinds that have natures that have nothing to do with the response to them of minds; they are as they are in themselves and relate as they do because of their natures. Necessary connections and what things are compatible or incompatible are determined by these mind-independent natures. Hence, there is a modality—the one composed of the natures of things in themselves—that is in the world yet has nothing to do with language or concepts. From this understanding arises a different conception of metaphysics, one on which its purpose is to make clear how things are in themselves and how these things relate. To be sure, this understanding raises deep epistemological questions (the most pressing of which is how the mind-independent nature of a thing can be known, when that thing can only be known via the mind), but this sort of question is posterior to the metaphysics.

The Criticism of Taylor's Contemporaries

The understanding of the world underlying Taylor's argument is the Aristotelian one. This is clear from his acknowledgment of necessary and sufficient—and *essential*—connections that are neither "logical" nor physical (1962a, 42, 43). I think there are compelling reasons to embrace this understanding, but for present purposes I merely accept it as correct. Given this understanding of the world, Taylor presumes that the modality relevant to metaphysical investigation is one based on the natures of things in themselves. This modality is not linguistic; moreover, despite not being based on causation nor any laws of nature, it is nonetheless fully in the world. It is, then, from this basis that Taylor argues that his familiar premises lead to fatalism. As noted above, this understanding of the world and the conception of metaphysics that accompanies it were at odds with the views prevailing when Taylor's argument appeared.

This argument purports to show that there is no contingency and, therefore, no agency and, a fortiori, no free action.

Presumably since it is concerns about one's personal freedom that make urgent recondite metaphysical discussions of contingency, Taylor presents the Aristotelian argument with a focus on its consequences for one's freedom. As a result, critical discussion of it has had this focus and so has been couched in terms of agency and free will rather than in the more general ones of contingency and its conditions.

The upshot of Taylor's argument is that at some imminent moment one of the states of affairs in every contradictory pair, s and $-s$, is impossible. Suppose it is s. The grounds that Taylor adduces for the claim that s is impossible is that a necessary condition for s, some state of affairs, n, does not occur. Since n is necessary for s, s *is impossible because some necessary condition of it does not exist*. If s is impossible, an agent lacks the power or ability to bring it about: one cannot do what is impossible.

One of the first criticisms of Taylor's argument, leveled by John Turk Saunders (1962a), is that it does not follow from the fact that a necessary condition of some state of affairs does not exist that one lacks the power or ability to bring that state of affairs about. So just as having in one's hands a violin is a necessary condition for playing a violin, from the fact that one does not have a violin in one's hands it does not follow that one lacks the power or ability to play. One has this ability—and so it is not impossible that one play—it is just that at some moments circumstances prevent the ability from being exercised. Accordingly, it is incorrect to conclude, merely on the grounds that a necessary condition for it fails to exist, that s is impossible. Insofar as one has the ability to bring about s and the ability to bring about $-s$, both are possible. Thus, there is, *pace* Taylor, contingency.

Taylor (1962b, 57) concedes Saunders's point: one can have the power or ability to bring about s despite a necessary condition for s failing to exist. Yet he disagrees with Saunders about its significance. Saunders maintains that it *follows* conceptually, or from the rules of English, that if an agent has the ability to bring about s (at moment m), then s is possible at m. Taylor holds that an agent might have such an ability and that it nevertheless be the case that s is impossible at m. Despite the ability, the possibility of s might be precluded by other features of the world.

Taylor's position leads Saunders (1962b) to charge that he is merely abusing language.[6] However, the real bone of contention is not linguistic; rather the issue here is fundamental disagreement about the modality operative in Taylor's argument. Saunders is presuming the relevant modality is linguistic-cum-conceptual; given the English language, the attribution of an ability to bring about s necessitates the possibility of s. Yet Taylor is basing his claims about what is possible on nonlinguistic features of the world; given these features, viz., the absence of a necessary condition for s, s is impossible—despite anyone's abilities. With such disagreement, Saunders fails even to engage Taylor's argument and so provides no reason for thinking it faulty.

Similar failure to engage with Taylor's Aristotelian argument—arising from the prevailing view that the only modalities pertinent to philosophy per se are linguistic—can be found in all the best-known critiques of Taylor by his contemporaries. Thus, Raziel Abelson (1963) maintains that Taylor "systematically equivocates" between two senses of modal terms like "necessary," "sufficient," "can," etc. Abelson assumes that these notions are either "logical," i.e., pertaining to language and concepts, or "causal," i.e., pertaining to the causes of things in the extralinguistic world.

According to Abelson, then, Taylor begins with the linguistic notion of necessity when he claims that some state of affairs, s, is a sufficient condition of another state of affairs, n. Given this notion, it is clearly true, if n, a necessary condition of s, does not occur, it is impossible that s does. If being unmarried is a necessary condition for being a bachelor, and one is married, then it is impossible that one is a bachelor. This is just a linguistic-cum-conceptual point and clearly holds. Yet Taylor goes on to make claims about states of affairs that are "logically unrelated"—states not connected by linguistic rules or concepts—and so it seems the modal terms in his argument cannot be construed in the "logical" sense.

If, however, the terms are not construed in this sense, Abelson maintains that Taylor cannot legitimately derive the strong conclusion that *s* is impossible if *n* does not exist. Abelson assumes that in the causal sense, if a necessary condition of *s* does not exist, all that follows is that *s does not* occur, not that *s* is *impossible*. If one does not have a violin in one's hands at a given moment, one does not play; it is not impossible that one play at that moment, for one might have picked up a violin just prior to it.

So Abelson accuses Taylor of equivocating, of deriving a strong modal conclusion from a modal notion too weak to support it. What Abelson fails to see is that Taylor is considering a modality that is neither logical nor causal. Taylor maintains that with this modality, one based on features of the world that are not merely physical or causal, the lack of a necessary condition for a state of affairs indeed renders that state impossible. Abelson simply fails to recognize the modality pertinent to Taylor's argument and, hence, just like Saunders, fails even to engage it.

Considerations very similar to Abelson's underlie the critique of Taylor by Charles D. Brown (1965). Relying on his ear, on what sounds colloquial, Brown draws a distinction between *necessary conditions of*, which are purely logical relations, and *necessary conditions for*, which are causal or physical and so relate features of the world. Taylor denies that the relations pertinent to his argument are logical or conceptual, so Brown maintains he must be using the causal notions. (Of course, Taylor explicitly denies his discussion has anything to do with causation—see above.) Yet if this is the case, Brown alleges, Taylor's conclusion that the absence of a necessary condition for a particular state of affairs renders that state impossible must be incorrect.

Brown allows that there can be states of affairs that are necessary conditions *of* prior states of affairs, but such relations, Brown assumes, must be purely logical. What Brown denies is that a subsequent state of affairs can be a necessary condition *for* a prior state of affairs. A subsequent state of affairs, *n*, cannot be a necessary condition for a prior one, *s*, since *n* occurs *after s*: *n* can exist and still not causally necessitate some preceding state of affairs, for an effect cannot precede its cause. Thus, *s* could occur or it could fail to occur regardless of *n*. It is, however, crucial to Taylor's argument that a state of affairs, *s*, at an imminent moment is impossible because a necessary condition *for* it, namely the existence of state of affairs, *n*, is lacking at a later moment. Thus, Brown concludes, Taylor's argument is fallacious.

What determines whether a certain state of affairs, *s*, occurs are the causal conditions prior to it—what happens subsequently to *s*, according to Brown, has nothing to do with whether *s* occurs and, thus, with whether *s* is possible. Taylor, however, is arguing that features of the world subsequent to *s* can render *s* impossible. But the relevant modality is not causal (nor conceptual), and Brown simply neglects to consider any other modality—indeed, Brown states: "I fail to see how 'necessary conditions *for*' can be legitimately interpreted other than causally" (1965, 129). So, yet again, there is a failure to engage with Taylor's argument.

In sum, Taylor's Aristotelian influences led him to recognize and take seriously a modality based on features of the world independent of language or concepts. Hence, one of the key assumptions of Taylor's argument that he leaves tacit is that the modality relevant to it is based on the natures of things in themselves. Such a basis seems to have been alien to his contemporaries; so strange indeed that the critiques appearing soon after Taylor's argument failed even to engage—let alone debunk—it.[7]

NECESSITY AND POSSIBILITY IN A TEMPORAL WORLD

After much attention in the first few years following its appearance, Taylor's fatalistic argument was less discussed. However, such a straightforward argument with a conclusion inimical to so familiar a conception of the world and one's place in it was hardly forgotten. Two decades after the spate of publications responding to Taylor, David Foster Wallace, dissatisfied with previous attempts to debunk the argument, made his own. Wallace's discussion is sophisticated and precocious yet still fails really to engage Taylor's Aristotelian argument. Nevertheless, it is important because Wallace's critique brings to the fore the crucial notion for illuminating not only Taylor's argument but contingency itself.

Wallace on Taylor

By the 1980s, when Wallace was considering Taylor, metaphysical inquiry had been sufficiently revived—through the efforts of Saul Kripke, Hilary Putnam, Alvin Plantinga, Roderick Chisholm, David Armstrong, and David Lewis, to name a few—that it was no longer simply taken for granted that the relevant modality in a philosophical context was linguistic. Consequently, Wallace recognizes the need at the outset of his critique to get clear on the modality relevant to Taylor's discussion. He determines that since Taylor obviously takes himself to be talking about the world itself—the realm of agency and free action—rather than how one speaks or thinks of it, the modality is not "logical," that is, linguistic-cum-conceptual. He states, then, that the modality and the "relations treated of here by Taylor must be regarded as physical and causal, not logical" (Wallace 1985, 147). As pointed out above, though, Taylor is explicit that his argument does not rely on any claims about the physical world and has nothing to do with causation.

Wallace is not unaware of this. Yet he insists that the relevant modality is physical-cum-causal "even though Taylor maintains, confusingly, that 'Our problem has been formulated without any reference whatever to causation' " (147).

Wallace's procrustean interpretation seems to come simply from his failure to recognize a modality that is fully in and about the world yet not based on conditions imposed by causality or physical relations in the material world (147–148). It is such a modality, based on the natures of things in themselves, that is operative in Taylor's discussion. Wallace, therefore, like Taylor's contemporary critics considered above, fails to appreciate from the start the nature of Taylor's project. Nonetheless, he examines, with more determination than his predecessors, modal connections that are genuinely in the world, and this enables one to discern the crux of Taylor's Aristotelian argument.

Wallace sees that the modality relevant to Taylor's discussion is supposed to be in the world, yet he is unable to recognize the Aristotelian understanding of reality and conception of metaphysics motivating Taylor. This leads Wallace to question how exactly the states of affairs in Taylor's argument are necessarily connected, and this, in turn, leads him to take up Brown's criticism of Taylor. Like Brown, Wallace thinks Taylor's argument is fallacious ultimately because Taylor conflates different notions of a necessary condition.

As discussed above, Brown holds there is a distinction between being a *necessary condition for* and being a *necessary condition of*; the former is a straightforward physical relation, the latter merely logical or conceptual. Wallace maintains that things in the extra-linguistic world may be necessary conditions *of* other such things but concurs with Brown that the two conditions impose different temporal relations on their relata. Whereas if n is a necessary condition *for* s, s and n must either occur simultaneously or n must occur prior to s; if n is a necessary condition *of* s, s must occur prior to n. To illustrate: if n (the presence of fuel) is a necessary condition *for s* (combustion occurring), n must occur prior to s—or the two states of affairs must be simultaneous, but if n (a sea battle's occurring) is a necessary condition of s (an order for a sea battle's being given), s must occur prior to n.

As Wallace interprets Taylor's argument, it requires one to consider whether a state of affairs, s, is possible in the absence of a necessary condition that occurs subsequent to it. Wallace, in agreement with Brown, thinks it obvious that s is impossible in the absence of a necessary condition (that is, precondition) *for* it but finds the case of an absent necessary condition *of s* less clear. The difficulty arises from considering a relation between states of affairs from distinct temporal perspectives, in particular, considering the modal status of s at moment m from a perspective *subsequent* to m at which the necessary condition of s is supposed to occur.

The Taylor Inequivalence

This line of discussion indicates that Wallace (like Brown before him) fails to acknowledge fully the premises of Taylor's argument. In the argument, Taylor assumes that the world in time is ontologically homogeneous; hence, whether a necessary condition of a state of affairs, s, occurs prior or subsequent to s simply makes no difference. It is, nonetheless, via this line that the crucial notion for illuminating Taylor's Aristotelian argument emerges. For through his effort to get clear on what to say about cases in which a necessary condition of a state of affairs at a particular moment subsequently fails to exist, Wallace notes an ambiguity in claims about the modal status of a feature of the world at a moment when evaluated from the perspective of a distinct moment. This ambiguity is of the utmost importance not only to Wallace's critique and dismissal of Taylor's argument but also to appreciating the argument.

The crux of Wallace's criticism of Taylor is that he fails to recognize distinct claims about the modal status of features of the world in time. According to Wallace, Taylor conflates:

(MT1) if at $m_2(-n)$, then at $m_1(-\text{Pos: } s)$

and

(MT2) if at $m_2(-n)$, then $-\text{Pos}(\text{at } m_1: s)$[8]

Wallace calls the distinction here the Taylor Inequivalence. The first claim states that if a certain state of affairs, n, does not occur at m_2, then at m_1, a prior moment, another state of affairs, s, is in itself not possible. The second claim states something different: if a certain state of affairs, n, does not occur at m_2, then it is not possible that at m_1 s occurs.

The differences here are subtle. (MT1) is the claim that the lack of n at m_2 has as a consequence that at a prior moment, m_1—from the perspective of that very moment itself—s is impossible; in other words, considering only how the world is at m_1, s could not be. But (MT2) is the claim that the lack of n at m_2 has as a consequence that it is impossible that s occur at m_1. This leaves open what exactly renders s impossible at m_1. There need be no reason to think that it is how things are at m_1 that makes s impossible—it is perhaps what goes on at other moments, e.g., the lack of n at m_2.

Wallace contends that Taylor becomes confused by the language in which he expresses his argument. He fails to distinguish these elusive differences between claims about the modal status of features of the world in time. Wallace asserts: "An analysis that can show that MT1 and MT2 are not equivalent, why they are not equivalent, that MT2 not MT1 follows from Taylor's argument, and that only MT1 would actually force fatalism on us, should represent a significant step toward solving the Taylor problem" (165).

Wallace draws out the differences between (MT1) and (MT2) with a colorful (if infelicitous) example. He supposes that a group of terrorists brings a nuclear weapon to Amherst College. The commander of this group has all the normal capacities of any healthy adult. He sits all day with his finger on the button that would detonate the weapon; the apparatus is in perfect working order. Yet he does not depress the button. A nuclear explosion on the Amherst campus yesterday would be sufficient for radiation in excess of 20 rads today, that is, radiation in excess of 20 rads today is a necessary condition of a nuclear explosion yesterday.

Now suppose that there is not radiation at Amherst today in excess of 20 rads. Two things might follow from this: in light of the connection between a nuclear explosion and the local level of radiation, from the lack of radiation today (i.e., at m_2) it might follow that there could not have been an explosion yesterday (i.e., at m_1). This is indeed a very natural and plausible conclusion. Or, what might also follow, given the lack of radiation today (at m_2), then yesterday (at m_1) a nuclear explosion was in itself impossible, that is, the lack of radiation today makes it the case that yesterday, considering it from the perspective of that very day itself, a nuclear explosion was impossible.

Wallace's Dismissal of Taylor's Fatalistic Argument

Wallace maintains that the second conclusion, unlike the first, is bizarre. It does not seem that the absence of some state of affairs, n (e.g., the presence of a certain level of radiation), at a later moment can constrain how things are at an earlier moment by making some other state of affairs, s (e.g., a nuclear explosion), in itself impossible at that moment. But if s is not in itself impossible, it could occur (or could have occurred) at that moment—despite -s actually occurring—and so there is contingency in the world.

Taylor's fatalistic argument is supposed to demonstrate that the absence of some state of affairs, *n*, that is a necessary condition of a state of affairs, *s*, at a previous moment, *m*, shows *s* is impossible at *m*. If this conclusion is understood as (MT1), then *s* is in itself impossible at *m*. Consequently, Taylor's argument shows that there is no contingency. But if the conclusion of the argument is understood as (MT2), *s* is not *in itself* impossible at *m*, and fatalism does not follow. Therefore, Wallace thinks if he can only show that (MT1) and (MT2) are inequivalent, then he has undermined Taylor's argument, for this provides a way of interpreting its conclusion that is perfectly compatible with contingency. One can accept all the premises of the argument without accepting fatalism.

Most of Wallace's subsequent discussion is taken up with a presentation of a formal system in which to codify interpretations of the two claims; this is supposed to "provide formal reasons for thinking that propositions such as [MT1 and MT2] are not equivalent" (177). But the formalism is really superfluous. (MT1) and (MT2) are both clearly legitimate and different claims that one can make about the modal features of the world in time. Wallace's informal example suffices to illustrate these differences. The formalism he presents merely provides a way of regimenting the two claims; if one does not grasp their differences—if one did not already know how to interpret them—the formal system would be of no help.[9] So one can grant that (MT1) and (MT2) are not equivalent.

Even granting this inequivalence, however, Wallace has not undermined Taylor's argument. He has indeed shown that there are two ways of understanding its conclusion, one consistent with contingency, one not. Were it the case that he and Taylor were making all the same assumptions, then Wallace's reading of the conclusion would show that fatalism does not validly follow from Taylor's argument's premises. But Wallace and Taylor are actually making incompatible assumptions about the nature of contingency; each is presupposing a totally different view of the modal features of the world in time. Given Taylor's view, the conclusion of his argument must be interpreted in line with (MT1); Wallace concedes that this leads to fatalism. Given Wallace's view, the conclusion of the argument may be interpreted in line with (MT2), and this is compatible with contingency. Therefore, it is on the truth of this fundamental and unstated assumption—regarding synchronic possibility—that the appropriate conclusion of Taylor's argument turns.

TWO METAPHYSICS OF CONTINGENCY

Wallace takes the modality relevant to Taylor's discussion to be physical-cum-causal, one based on those connections among things determined by physics or the laws of nature. He maintains that what Taylor's argument demonstrates is that the absence of some necessary consequence of a certain state of affairs, s, shows only that s *did not* occur at an earlier moment, m—it could not have occurred *given the laws of nature and the absence of its necessary consequence*. According to Wallace, the argument does not show that s is in itself *impossible* at m. Indeed, Wallace takes for granted, considering s in itself, insofar as s itself is compatible with the laws of nature, that although s did not occur at m, it could have. This is precisely what Taylor rejects.

Synchronic Possibility

Taylor assumes that if s does not (or did not) occur at m, then s could not occur (could not have occurred) at m. This is not, however, merely to presume fatalism. Rather, it is to accept a different view of contingency than the one presupposed by Wallace and all Taylor's other critics. The different views turn on the modal status of features of the world at a moment considered at that moment. The key issue is whether at a given moment, m, considering some state of affairs, s, at m, whether s—at m—could be otherwise than it in fact is, that is, whether at m there are nonactualized possibilities. The issue here, in other words, is whether there is synchronic possibility in the world.

Among the ancients and medievals, it appears to have been universally accepted that there was no synchronic possibility: at each existent moment everything must be just as it is at that moment.[10] The notion that there were unactualized possibilities at a moment was revolutionary. It is thought to have been introduced by John Duns Scotus in the fourteenth century.[11] The notion naturally accompanied discussions of modality in the early- to mid-twentieth century, where the only modality thought to be relevant to philosophy per se was linguistic-cum-conceptual. It is certainly consistent with how we speak or conceive of the world that things be otherwise than how they are at a given moment: although I wear a white shirt at m, it is not a contradiction in terms or conceptually incoherent to hold that I wear a blue shirt at m.[12]

Moreover, the notion of synchronic possibility also naturally accompanies talk of *possible worlds*, which since the end of the 1960s has been widespread. Regardless of how they are conceived—as maximally consistent sets of sentences or propositions, as properties the actual world might have, as complete concrete universes—it seems plausible that there are possible worlds in which things are otherwise than they are at this very moment. Thus, there is a maximally consistent set of sentences that represents me as now wearing a blue shirt, though I wear a white one, or perhaps there is someone quite like me in some other concrete world now wearing a blue shirt.

Possibilities *at* a Moment Versus Possibility *from* a Moment

Given the notion of synchronic possibility, two very different pictures of how possibility is located in the world arise; depending on this notion, then, there are two distinct metaphysics of contingency.

If one accepts synchronic possibility, one gets an account of contingency on which at every moment that exists there is an array of distinct possibilities. Possibility is located at each actual moment: *at* each moment reality could be otherwise than it in fact is. On this picture, speaking figuratively, modal reality overlays temporal reality; possibilities burgeon throughout time.

If one denies synchronic possibility, at every moment that exists things must be just as they are. At no moment does non-actualized possibility exist. Thus, insofar as there is unactualized possibility, it begins where the world in time ends, and, consequently, there is not a never-ending succession of moments each of which is equally real. Presumably, there is now no subsequent moment. Everything must exist at any moment it does and just as it is; hence, all true claims about the temporal world are necessarily true. Nevertheless, all this is compatible with contingency, for the world could be ever so many different ways subsequent to this moment: possibility arises not *at* this moment but *from* it. There is more to the actual world because it could become more in time. On this picture, speaking figuratively, modal reality abuts temporal reality; the future is the realm of possibility.

Taylor does not explicitly deny synchronic possibility—indeed, he does not mention the notion at all—yet it is clear that he rejects unactualized possibilities at a moment. Thus, his rejection of synchronic possibility is a second key assumption of Taylor's fatalistic argument that he leaves tacit, accompanying the assumption that the modality relevant to the argument is based on the natures of things in themselves.

The best evidence that Taylor rejects synchronic possibility is that Taylor's argument is obviously Aristotelian, and Aristotle is explicit in his discussion of time and modality that he rejects synchronic possibility. Consider: "What is, necessarily is, when it is; and what is not, necessarily is not, when it is not."[13] Aristotle's discussion here is the inspiration for and basis of Taylor's ruminations on fatalism. Moreover, Taylor (1963, 85) takes himself to be presenting the same sort of argument that disturbed St. Augustine and Boethius. Such an argument would bring with it the ancient presuppositions about the nature of reality, and, as noted above, one of these presuppositions is that there is no synchronic possibility. Last, given the assumption that there is no synchronic possibility—and a modality based on the natures of things in themselves—Taylor's Aristotelian argument is undeniably valid. (I defend this claim below.)

It is as clear that Taylor's critics are assuming there is synchronic possibility as it is that Taylor assumes there is not. When considering the Taylor Inequivalence in the context of his colorful example, Wallace claims that Taylor takes it to be an upshot of his argument that at some moment, m, when the commander of the terrorists sat with his finger on the button that would detonate the nuclear weapon at Amherst and did *not* depress the button, that it was *impossible* for him to do so. To this, Wallace responds: "this is clearly just plain wrong: I have constructed the case in just such a way that under any halfway reasonable definition of situational physical possibility [i.e., the modality relevant to the argument] it is physically possible at [m] for the explosion to occur at [m]" (171).

If, however, there is no synchronic possibility and there is no explosion at m, then it is indeed impossible for there to be an explosion at m. Thus, Wallace asserts—without any consideration—that a key assumption of Taylor's argument, one crucial not only to understanding that argument but also Taylor's position and motivation more generally, is "clearly wrong," not even "halfway reasonable." It is no wonder, then, that Wallace dismisses Taylor's argument as fallacious!

The present point—that Wallace takes for granted synchronic possibility—might be obscured by several comments he makes in the course of distinguishing the physical-cum-causal modality he thinks is relevant to Taylor's argument from the modality he thinks typically underlies metaphysical discussions. The notion of possibility accompanying the latter is, according to Wallace, understood "in terms of a synchronic relation between alternative, simultaneous possible 'worlds' . . . while I will be arguing that physical possibility is best understood as a *diachronic* relation of compatibility under causal laws between sets of conditions as the condition-sets stand in appropriate relations through time" (177, see also 180–181). Despite appearances, this quotation actually corroborates the present point. Wallace is proposing a restriction on "logical" or "alethic" modality, the notion that he thinks underlies contemporary metaphysical discussions, because he thinks this notion is not sensitive to changing features of the world. I believe this is mistaken, a vestige—which Wallace accepts uncritically—of the prevailing view for several decades that the modality relevant to philosophy is linguistic-cum-conceptual. But the "logical" modality that Wallace proposes to restrict, by his own acknowledgment, includes synchronic possibility, so it is part of the framework he employs in attempting to undermine Taylor's argument. The importance of synchronic possibility to Wallace's thinking about how possibility is in the world is apparent from the "visual apparatus" he presents to illustrate his discussion: although the focus is on the relations among worlds at moments, an essential feature of these moments is that there are many possibilities at any given one (Wallace 1985, 184–186).

Therefore, Wallace summarily rejects, as one that could not be right, a key assumption of Taylor's argument. He was not alone in doing this. Abelson, Taylor's contemporary critic, notes that it follows from Taylor's assumptions that "since every event is a necessary and sufficient condition for itself, the nonoccurrence of an event would render that event impossible while the occurrence would render it necessary" (Abelson 1963, 82). Abelson concludes that this result arises from fallacious reasoning and leads trivially to fatalism. But he is incorrect on both counts. The result is not a consequence of Taylor's argument; it is, rather, a presupposition of it—it is the assumption that there is no synchronic possibility. This assumption, however, leads to fatalism only if one rejects the alternative metaphysics of contingency (the one that Taylor, in the end, accepts). Others, like Brown (1965, 127), who charged that Taylor begs the question of fatalism at the outset of his discussion were in error for similar reasons.

The Proper Interpretation of Taylor's Argument Turns on the Notion of Synchronic Possibility

Taylor's denial of synchronic possibility, inspired and motivated by Aristotle, is the key both to appreciating his fatalistic argument and also to understanding his attitude toward it. He was quite confident in the argument and certain of its validity (see Taylor 1962b, 1963, 1964). As presented, the focus of the argument is on the necessary connections between states of affairs. Underlying the argument, though, is the notion of synchronic possibility.

Bearing these points in mind, the crux of the argument can be presented in a form that is transparent and simple: Suppose that there is no synchronic possibility. The way things are at a certain moment, m, must be as they are, and so a given state of affairs, s_1, at m is necessary. If this is so, and there is a necessary connection (based, one may assume, on the very natures of the things in themselves) between s_1 and another state of affairs, s_2, at a different moment, then s_2 must exist at that moment. The reasoning here: Necessarily p and necessarily (if p, then q), therefore necessarily

q is clearly valid—indeed it is taken as an axiom of any standard system of modal logic.

This view of the argument not only makes patent its validity but also provides the means for simplifying the long and complicated dialectic surrounding it. Taylor's contemporaries focused their criticism on the necessary connections between states of affairs that are crucial to Taylor's argument. Beginning with the linguistic-cum-conceptual modality, which they presumed was the only legitimate one, they argued in different ways that these necessary connections were problematic. Thus, Saunders maintains that it does not follow from the lack of a necessary condition for some state of affairs, s, that one cannot bring s about; Abelson and Brown maintain that the necessary connections Taylor relies on are illegitimate because of equivocation or some other sort of confusion. Because of their failure to recognize the modality operative in Taylor's argument, such criticisms failed even to engage it. However, the more important point for present purposes is that with this focus on the necessary connections employed in the argument, the issue of synchronic possibility does not become salient.

With the revival of metaphysical inquiry and the recognition of the philosophical legitimacy of different modalities, some of which are fully in the world, i.e., *not* linguistic-cum-conceptual, consideration of the argument shifted from its crucial necessary connections between states of affairs, which now seemed less alien, to what is the case—or must be the case—at a particular moment. Wallace takes it for granted that at any given moment there are myriad unactualized possible states of affairs. Presuming this, then, it is *not* the case that at a certain moment, m, a given state of affairs, s_1, is necessary. If this is so, one can concede a necessary connection between s_1 and another state of affairs, s_2, at a different moment, and still it does not follow that s_2 is necessary. Indeed, it *clearly* does not follow that s_2 is necessary. This line of reasoning explains Wallace's attitude toward Taylor's argument: given Wallace's assumptions, it is fallacious and obviously so.

Therefore, assuming there can be necessary connections between states of affairs in the world,[14] if one accepts that there are synchronic possibilities, as Wallace—and many other contemporary philosophers do—Taylor's Aristotelian argument is clearly invalid; if one denies synchronic possibility, as Taylor and the ancients and most medievals did, the argument is clearly valid. Regardless of whether there is synchronic possibility, one can accept contingency, nonactualized possibility in the world. There are, however, two very different metaphysics of contingency depending on whether there is synchronic possibility. If there is, things now could be otherwise than they in fact are; if there is not, things must be just as they are (and were) though the world could be different—at a subsequent moment. Rejecting synchronic possibility, Taylor presupposed an unfamiliar way of understanding how possibility is in the world and then shows, with his argument, that this way is incompatible with contingency given certain popular assumptions. Taylor is not guilty of any bad reasoning. He might, however, be charged with fostering confusion by failing to articulate the Aristotelian presuppositions regarding modality and metaphysics and synchronic possibility underlying his discussion.

CONCLUSION

What emerges from examining Taylor's argument is that there are two different ways of locating possibility in the world, two different metaphysics of contingency. On one, there is possibility *at* a moment; on the other, there is possibility *from* a moment. If the former view is correct, Taylor's fatalistic argument is invalid—if the latter is correct, the argument is valid, and, hence, in order to accept contingency, one must reject some of the popular assumptions on which the argument is based. Yet either way there is contingency: one need have no fears regarding fatalism.

One should not presume that just because there is an assumption one could make, viz., accepting synchronic possibility, from which it follows that Taylor's argument is invalid, that this assumption is true. The assumption entails a particular metaphysics of contingency. There are, however, two incompatible metaphysics of contingency—the question of which is correct remains. Given its connection to modality and the world in time and truth, this is a question of profound and far-reaching metaphysical importance.

Taylor (like Aristotle) merely takes for granted that there is no synchronic possibility; his critics, including Wallace, merely presume there is. Therefore, Taylor's argument itself and all the critiques of it really provide no insight into this issue. To determine the correct account of contingency, one must go beyond this argument. Above, I stated that I thought the conclusions about the world in time and truth about the world that Taylor, following Aristotle, draws from his argument are correct. This is because I believe there are compelling reasons to reject synchronic possibility. This is not the place for a full discussion of these issues,[15] but in closing, I present some of these reasons and then ameliorate the conclusion that there are *not* many moments of time, all of which are equally real, and that it is *not* the case that every proposition whatsoever is either true or, if not true, false.

Reasons for Thinking There Is No Synchronic Possibility

The first thing to note is how odd the assumption is that right now things could be other than they actually are. As things are, I now wear a white shirt. It is certainly natural to think that with respect to what I am wearing at this moment reality is complete—is *full*— and, therefore, must be as it is. Yet if there is synchronic possibility, it is possible that I now wear a blue shirt. This might seem plausible, for one might suppose it possible that earlier today I put on a blue shirt (rather than a white one). However, this sort of consideration provides no *grounds* for thinking that right now things could be other than they are, for it merely presupposes synchronic possibility: one who advances it presumes that at the very moment at which I actually put on a white shirt I might have put on a blue one.

It is difficult to see how one could provide grounds for the claim that there is synchronic possibility. Indeed, to my knowledge, not a single contemporary philosopher has provided any reason whatsoever for this claim—yet that there is synchronic possibility is universally accepted (to my knowledge). The considerations Duns Scotus adduces for synchronic possibility when introducing the notion are based on doctrinal assumptions, ones that many today would find implausible or otherwise objectionable (see again Normore 2002). Of course, if one believes that the source of necessity and possibility is ultimately how the minds of conscious beings interact with the world (and, hence, that the only legitimate philosophical modality is linguistic-cum-conceptual), then synchronic possibility is corollary. But such a position is much less accepted in contemporary metaphysics than it was throughout the twentieth century. I believe that philosophers have simply failed to recognize that when this position is dismissed, so is any reason for accepting synchronic possibility. Moreover, the reliance on and familiarity of talk of possible worlds, which abet the acceptance of synchronic possibility, has obscured the fact that this acceptance is entirely unmotivated.

These negative considerations are not meant to be a strong argument against the claim that there is synchronic possibility; rather, they are meant to expose the tenuousness of this claim. I present now a positive argument against synchronic possibility. The combination of this argument with the foregoing considerations seems to me to provide a compelling reason to reject synchronic possibility and, hence, to accept the metaphysics of contingency that eschews this notion.

Suppose at moment *m* there is a cat before one. At *m*, the cat is white. It is plausible that the cat, being an instance of a certain kind of thing, has essential features, features it must have in virtue of being a cat (perhaps, being a living thing, being a mammal, being extended). It is implausible that its color is one of these essential features. There are cats of many different colors, and this cat could surely survive and be grey. Considering only the cat, then, it might seem that although at *m* the cat is white, it is possible that at *m* the cat is grey (or at *m* the cat is possibly grey)—there is, after all, nothing in its nature that precludes it from being grey at *m*. However, there is more in the world to consider.

At moment *m*, the world is a unique and particular way, e.g., with respect to the color of the cat. If the cat and its nature cannot ground and explain this particularity—and they cannot if the cat could be white and could be grey—then, presumably, there is something else in the world that can. Perhaps it is the *state of affairs* of the cat being white at *m* or the cat's particular whiteness at *m* (that is, a *trope* or *mode*) or the *simple fact* that the cat is white at *m*. Whatever it is, whatever is the ontological grounds of this particular feature of the world at *m*, it is not feasible to think that it is compatible with the nature of this thing that the cat be grey at *m*. Thus, for example, it does not seem that the state of affairs of the cat being white at *m* could exist yet it be possible that the cat be grey at *m*—the very nature of *this* entity, unlike the cat itself, seems to preclude the possibility.

The example generalizes: insofar as the world has a unique nature at each moment, and insofar as there are grounds for and explanation of the particular features that underlie this uniqueness, there are entities to whose nature it is incompatible that the world be otherwise at that moment. Therefore, there are in the world things that exclude synchronic possibility.

Why the Resulting Picture of the World Is Not So Bad

As noted above, the upshot of this conclusion is that if there is contingency, then temporal reality is not ontologically homogeneous, and every proposition is not either true or false. I find neither consequence unfeasible.

If there are not many moments of time, all with the same ontological status, then, assuming that this moment, now, is real, there are significant ontological differences between the present and the future and past. But it is not at all farfetched to think that one differs ontologically from dinosaurs and Napoleon or from one's great-great-great-great-grandchildren and Martian outposts; one exists, whereas the others do not in any sense. There are many developed positions in the metaphysics of time that accept such ontological heterogeneity in temporal reality, so this thesis can hardly be regarded as extreme. I myself defend a presentist view on which, though the past is real, there are no past moments—no past entities whatsoever—and on which there are no future entities and, hence, no facts about what will be (Fiocco 2007).

Even less problematic is the consequence that not all propositions are either true or false. If this is so, then some propositions are indeterminate; they lack a truth value. Indeterminacy is a phenomenon recognized in connection to many issues in the philosophy of language, in physics, and in metaphysics. Here, then, is another. To say that indeterminacy is unproblematic as a consequence of contingency is certainly not to suggest that the phenomenon, in its multiplicity, is amenable to any simple or definitive account but only to acknowledge that it is a genuine phenomenon. To deny it outright seems to me farfetched; the assumption of bivalence for all propositions seems somewhat naïve or myopic. Thus, if contingency requires it, one has merely another appearance of indeterminacy to consider.

In the end, the value of considering Taylor's Aristotelian argument is that it brings to light two different metaphysics of contingency. Examining these, one ends up with a view on which there is contingency yet no contingent features of the world (or claims about it). Reality is such that it contains the capacity for change and evolution without any feature being able to be otherwise than it in fact is. This leaves one with a view of temporal reality on which there is nothing but possibility after this moment, now. Far from being objectionable, this view seems to be both true and just the way any self who aspires to free expression and growth would hope the world to be.

NOTES

1. See Taylor (1962a, 43). "If any state of affairs is sufficient for, though logically unrelated to, the occurrence of some further condition at the same time or any other time, then the former cannot occur without the latter occurring."

2. This view of temporal reality would have been familiar to Taylor's contemporaries from, e.g., Russell (1915), Williams (1951), Smart (1955), and Quine (1960). It is familiar to contemporary readers from more recent discussions, such as Sider (2001), Mellor (1998, 1981), Lewis (1986), and Oaklander (1984).

3. In particular, the section "Considerations of Time." See Taylor (1962a, 47–48).

4. See, in particular, Taylor (1957).

5. This idea, that a true representation is *made true* by some feature of reality, is widely accepted in contemporary metaphysics. For defense of the claim that every true proposition must, on pain of contradiction, be made true, see Fiocco (2013). It is an idea that seems to have been accepted by both Taylor (1963, 87) and Wallace (1985, 175).

6. For related criticism, see Aune (1962, 71) and Makepeace (1962).

7. From his responses (Taylor 1962b, 1963, 1964), it seems Taylor himself was not aware of how out of step he was with his colleagues and, thus, that the source of their disagreement was radical: very different

understandings of the nature of reality and ancillary views of metaphysics. In his contribution to the present volume, William Hasker also suggests that confusion regarding modality, endemic to that period of analytic philosophy, is relevant to evaluating the objections of Taylor's contemporaries to his Aristotelian argument. See chapter 1.

8. See Wallace (1985, 164). I have changed Wallace's notation to bring it in line with my presentation of Taylor's argument above.

9. Hasker makes a similar point in his contribution to this volume when he suggests that Wallace may be overlooking the fact that "*formal logical systems rest on intuitive foundations*" (italics are Hasker's).

10. For discussion, see Knuuttila (1993, chaps. 1–2).

11. See Knuuttila (1993, chap. 4) and Normore (2002).

12. Though, of course, it would be a contradiction in terms to hold that I wear a white shirt and a blue, i.e., nonwhite, shirt at m (assuming I wear but one shirt).

13. Note that Aristotle goes on to say: "But not everything that is, is, necessarily is; and not everything that is not, necessarily is not. For to say that everything that is, is of necessity, when it is, is not the same as saying unconditionally that it is of necessity" (*De Interpretatione*, chap. 9, 19a). Thus, denying synchronic possibility is not in itself to reject contingency.

14. One should note that none of Taylor's critics give any reason for denying this assumption. Rejecting it is merely part of the view that the only modality relevant to philosophy per se is linguistic-cum-conceptual. This view, so dominant throughout the twentieth century, is no longer orthodox.

15. I consider them in much more detail in Fiocco (manuscript).

REFERENCES

Abelson, R. 1963. "Taylor's Fatal Fallacy." *Philosophical Review* 72, no. 1. Reprinted in Cahn and Eckert 2011, 79–83. Citations refer to the reprint.

Aristotle. 1987. *De Interpretatione*. In *A New Aristotle Reader*, ed. J. Ackrill. Princeton, N.J.: Princeton University Press.

Aune, B. 1962. "Fatalism and Professor Taylor." *Philosophical Review* 71, no. 4. Reprinted in Cahn and Eckert 2011, 69–78. Citations refer to the reprint.

Brown, C. D. 1965. "Fallacies in Taylor's 'Fatalism.'" *Journal of Philosophy* 62, no. 13. Reprinted in Cahn and Eckert 2011, 127–132. Citations refer to the reprint.

Cahn, S., and M. Eckert, eds. 2011. *Fate, Time, and Language: An Essay on Free Will*, by David Foster Wallace. New York: Columbia University Press.

Fiocco, M. O. 2007. "A Defense of Transient Presentism." *American Philosophical Quarterly* 44: 191-212

——. 2013. "An Absolute Principle of Truthmaking." *Grazer Philosophische Studien* 88: 1-31.

——. Manuscript. "Truth, Modality, and Time."

Hasker, W. 2014. "David Foster Wallace and the Fallacies of Fatalism." Chapter 1 of the present volume.

Knuuttila, S. 1993. *Modalities in Medieval Philosophy*. London: Routledge.

Lewis, D. 1986. *On the Plurality of Worlds*. Oxford: Basil Blackwell.

Makepeace, P. 1962. "Fatalism and Ability II." *Analysis* 23. Reprinted in Cahn and Eckert 2011, 61–64. Citations refer to the reprint.

Mellor, D. H. 1981. *Real Time*. Cambridge: Cambridge University Press.

——. 1998. *Real Time II*. London: Routledge.

Normore, C. 2002. "Duns Scotus's Modal Theory." In *The Cambridge Companion to Duns Scotus*, ed. T. Williams. Cambridge: Cambridge University Press.

Oaklander, L. N. 1984. *Temporal Relations and Temporal Becoming: A Defense of a Russellian Theory of Time*. Lanham, Md.: University Press of America.

Quine, W. V. 1960. *Word and Object*. Cambridge, Mass.: MIT Press.

Russell, B. 1915. "On the Experience of Time." *The Monist* 25: 212–233.

Saunders, J. T. 1962a. "Professor Taylor on Fatalism." *Analysis* 23, no. 1. Reprinted in Cahn and Eckert 2011, 53–55. Citations refer to the reprint.

——. 1962b. "Fatalism and Linguistic Reform." *Analysis* 23. Reprinted in Cahn and Eckert 2011, 65–68. Citations refer to the reprint.

Sider, T. 2001. *Four-Dimensionalism: An Ontology of Persistence and Time*. Oxford: Oxford University Press.

Smart, J. 1955. "Spatialising Time." *Mind* 64: 239–241.

Taylor, R. 1957. "The Problem of Future Contingencies." *Philosophical Review* 66, no. 1. Reprinted as an appendix to Cahn and Eckert 2011, 223–252. Citations refer to the reprint.

——. 1962a. "Fatalism." *Philosophical Review* 71, no. 1. Reprinted in Cahn and Eckert 2011, 41–51. Citations refer to the reprint.

——. 1962b. "Fatalism and Ability." *Analysis* 23, no. 2. Reprinted in Cahn and Eckert 2011, 57–59. Citations refer to the reprint.

——. 1963. "A Note on Fatalism." *Philosophical Review* 72, no. 4. Reprinted in Cahn and Eckert 2011, 85–88. Citations refer to the reprint.

——. 1964. "Comment." *Journal of Philosophy* 61, no. 10. Reprinted in Cahn and Eckert 2011, 107–110. Citations refer to the reprint.

Wallace, D. F. 1985. "Richard Taylor's 'Fatalism' and the Semantics of Physical Modality." Honors Thesis, Amherst College. In Cahn and Eckert 2011, 141–216.

Williams, D. C. 1951. "The Myth of Passage." *Journal of Philosophy* 48: 457–472.

4

FATALISM, TIME TRAVEL, AND SYSTEM J

MAUREEN ECKERT

F atalists regard the future like the past. Time travelers regard the past like the future. This mirroring of the fatalist and time traveler suggests that there is some kind of common ground between them—but what is it? According to the fatalist, there is nothing now we can do to influence future events. Meanwhile, the time traveler can do things to influence the past. We may prefer the time traveler to the fatalist—being a Time Lord promises considerably more adventure than necessarily having to do everything that one does. Yet, both positions seem counterintuitive about whatever it is we can and cannot do, past and future. In the debate spurred by Richard Taylor's fatalism argument, the connection between fatalism and time travel begins to take shape in Taylor's response to the "Ability Criticism." The first section of this paper reviews this development of the issue. In the second section, we examine David Lewis's analysis and dissolution of the Grandfather Paradox, which further clarifies the connection. The third section of this paper examines how David Foster Wallace's critical response to Taylor's fatalist argument avoids the pitfalls of the earlier Ability Criticism. The semantic system he develops, System J, provides precision to Lewis's more general account of how a time traveler *can* act in the past without risking contradiction. We will see, in the final section, that the metaphysical commitments of System J would shut down *actual* time travel along with fatalism. Their initial mirroring turns on a common conceptual flaw.

FATALISM AND TIME TRAVEL ON THE CHEAP: THE ABILITY CRITICISM

In his "Note on Fatalism," Richard Taylor assesses the "Ability Criticism," an attack against the fifth premise of his fatalist argument. This premise reads: "Fifth, we presuppose that no agent *can* perform any given act if there is lacking, at the same or any other time, some condition necessary for the occurrence of that act."[1] The group of critics concerned, including Aune, Saunders, and Abelson, claim that an agent *can*, in fact, perform actions in the absence of a condition necessary for it to be accomplished. This is the case when an agent's abilities are concerned—hence the Ability Criticism. I can swim, for example, if it is the case I have learned how to do so and practiced it to proficiency—I am able to swim. I may be lacking some condition necessary to swim, e.g., being in a filled swimming pool, but it is true that "I can swim" in this sense.

According to Taylor, the Ability Criticism conflates three distinct notions: (1) what is within one's power to do given external circumstances, (2) what is possible for one to do, and (3) what is within one's ability to do given internal circumstances. This conflation, for Taylor, is significant because his argument is unaffected by (3), the individual "ability/skills" rendering. Even if I possess the *ability* to swim, it remains impossible to swim without necessary conditions being met (e.g., a present body of water in which to swim), and is it not within my power to exercise my ability in the absence of a necessary condition. Moreover, if the "can" of Taylor's fifth premise is understood as meaning "ability," there is a hidden cost. Reducing the notions of "possibility" and "what is within one's power" to "ability" for the sake of solving fatalism entails that abilities would then override possibility and doing whatever is within one's power generally. If the *ability* to swim, even lacking necessary conditions, liberates us from fatalism about future contingent events, it simultaneously allows us to change the past—what *is possible* and what *is in our power to do* no longer constrain our abilities. Contingent events that have happened in the past could be undone by what we can do—*as abilities*. Time travel comes much too cheaply if the ability criticism is taken seriously. Taylor states:

> Remarks upon what one may or may not have the ability to do, in the usual skill sense of ability, have no relevance to this problem at all. Not one of my critics has seen this. Nor have they seen that the very refutations they give of my fatalism about the future would work just as well to prove that we should not be fatalists about the past. I described a fatalist, however, simply as a man who looks upon the future the way we all look upon the past, so far as concerns what it is and what it is not within his power to do. If anyone wanted to show that we should not be fatalists about the past, that it is to some extent now up to us what happens yesterday, and so on, he could find all his arguments in the remarks of my critics, needing only to change a few tenses.[2]

Taylor notes that we are all fatalists about the past (the fatalist merely treats the future as we all consider the past).[3] The conflation of possibility, what is within one's power to do, and abilities leads to an unacceptable result—the ability to change the past by way of abilities. Disambiguating the senses of "can" in Taylor's fifth premise permits the fatalist argument to go through. In this way, Taylor dispenses with the Ability Criticism.

Taylor's response to the Ability Criticism nevertheless leaves some lingering concerns. He notes that there are three distinct senses of "can" that his critics conflate: (1) what is within one's power to do, (2) what is possible for one to do, and (3) what is within one's ability to do. Disambiguating the sense of "can" in the premise so that it does not regard an agent's abilities and skill sets (3) still leaves open what is going on with the distinctions he makes in (1) and (2). What is possible logically is much, much broader than what happens to be in one's power to do. Local, physical circumstances are relevant to what is or is not within one's power, as should be expected since it is the status of future contingent statements under consideration and not *all possibilities*. What is in one's power to do is a subclass of what is possible, but one must avoid conflating (1) and (2), as cases of what is possible (1) far outstrip whatever is in one's power to do (2). Thus, there remains some leverage for critically responding to premise five of Taylor's fatalist argument. David Foster Wallace exploits this remaining ambiguity in his attack on the fatalist argument, disambiguating these two remaining senses of "can" through distinguishing between physical possibility and what he terms "situational physical possibility." More will be said on Wallace's insight and metaphysical solution in the section "Wallace's System J," below.

Additionally, Taylor's response to the Ability Criticism relies on an intuitive notion of the past that can be challenged. We may all be fatalists about the past—except when we aren't. Science-fiction writers have not viewed the past fatalistically, as fans of *Doctor Who* might note. Contemporary physicists have seriously debated the theoretical possibility of time travel. Most importantly for our purposes, anyone arguing philosophically for the possibility of time travel, especially time travel into the past, must disambiguate (1) what is within one's power to do from (2) what is possible for one to do when constructing an account. As Taylor diagnoses the problem, conflating individual ability with what is possible for one to do and with what is in one's power to do provides a cheap and unconvincing route to time travel. One's abilities do not allow anyone to change the past. The time-traveling "ability" has to be more than merely a skill, as Taylor claims. David Lewis's assessment of the Grandfather Paradox in his argument for the possibility of time travel illustrates this condition.

TIME TRAVEL AND FATALISM ON THE CHEAP: DAVID LEWIS ON THE GRANDFATHER PARADOX

If a time traveler, Sarah, were to travel back in time two generations, *can* she kill her own grandfather? It would seem that, on the one hand, if she has successfully traveled back in time, causally interacting with the world at that time, and she is in the right location with a weapon at hand, there is nothing *at that time* that would prevent her from killing her grandfather. On the other hand, if, at that time, she were able to kill her own grandfather, she would then eliminate a necessary condition for her existence—there would be no future Sarah that *can* travel back in time to commit the act in question. The question of whether the time traveler Sarah can kill her grandfather appears to give rise to a contradiction. Time-traveling Sarah both can and cannot kill her grandfather. This "Grandfather Paradox" presents an obstacle to the notion that time travel to the past is possible. In "The Paradoxes of Time Travel," David Lewis attempts to dissolve this paradox with the intention of showing that it is possible.[4] Crucial in his analysis is an ambiguity also noted by Taylor: there are two senses of what a time traveler *can* do.

For Lewis, a time traveler arriving back in time before her own birth, able to interact causally with the environment and to be in the right place at the right moment with the right weapon, "has what it takes" to kill her own grandfather.[5] Lewis calls this way of tracking the time traveler's local actions "personal time." Personal time essentially moves with the time traveler such that she experiences her "now" wherever she happens to be in terms of the line of "objective time." Traveling back in time, she is objectively in the past, but it is her personal-time present. A Lewisian time traveler's "having what it takes" at the local, personal level of time corresponds to what Taylor calls having something "within one's power to do." With these phrases, both philosophers refer to the relevant contextual, situational details necessary to carry out an action. It is within Sarah's power to kill her grandfather in her personal time. But is it *possible?* Like Taylor, Lewis also distinguishes a broader kind of possibility from the contextual, situational sense of being able to do something. The broader range of facts about a time traveler—one that is inclusive of the whole chain of events that leads up to the time traveler's trip back to the past—excludes the possibility of killing one's own grandfather. These two ways of conceiving what a time traveler can do dissolves the paradox. He states: "You can reasonably choose the narrower delineation, and say that he can; or the wider delineation, and say that he can't. But choose. What you mustn't do is waver, say in the same breath that he both can and can't, and then claim that this contradiction proves that time travel is impossible."[6]

Lewis's diagnosis of this equivocation in what we mean by "can" in the time-traveler case applies to fatalism. For Lewis, the sleight of meaning rests in taking irrelevant facts as relevant facts. In other words, the fatalist argues it is necessary that we do what we do (and don't do what we can't do) by claiming that irrelevant facts about the future are relevant facts about the past. The time traveler has it within her power to kill her grandfather when narrowly and contextually considered. This maps to an ordinary sense of what we mean when we say we can do something. Shift the context such that we include all of the future events up through the time traveler's trip into the past as part of the context, and she cannot. She is, apparently, "fated" not to be able to do so. The Grandfather Paradox disguises this same shift in context operating in the fatalist's perspective. "We are unlikely to be fooled by the fatalist's methods of disguise in this case, or other ordinary cases," Lewis states. "But in cases of time travel, precognition, or the like, we're on less familiar ground, so it may take less of a disguise to fool us."[7] The fatalist exploits the context of objective time in order to determine (for once and for all) what we can and cannot do at the local level of personal time.

Lewis's dissolution of the Grandfather Paradox might leave some residual dissatisfaction. Personal and objective times are nevertheless in tension. One might suspect that a time traveler who can, in the narrow situational sense, kill her own grandfather is up to something that isn't merely logically off (contradictory) and certainly ethically off but also "metaphysically off." This latter oddness may be hard to tease out, although it seems clear that the time-traveling grandfather killer can very radically change the past, thus altering the physical chain of events in some real sense, if she really can kill her grandfather. The strongest way to address this radical alteration of the physical world is through the notion of branching time. According to Lewis, in such a scenario we find branches of time at which the grandfather is killed, others where he is not, but never one in which he both is and is not killed.[8] We still have a consistent story, one in which the time traveler appears and kills her grandfather in one branch while in other branches of time she does not. The consistency of each story depends upon tracking the time traveler's personal time in any given temporal branching. Why can't a time traveler succeed in preventing her own birth? For Lewis, insofar as we track this time traveler's (admittedly) unusual story along a branch of time, there is nothing to block it merely because it is so unusual. There is no contradictory branch, but this does not mean that things are quite normal along some branches of time.

The highly unusual sort of story seems to entail an abrogation of the situational physical causal chain of events that brought the time traveler into existence. Time-traveler Sarah can kill her grandfather in 1938 when she has traveled back to 1938 insofar as all the right circumstances are in place. We can grant this to Lewis. Yet the right circumstances were also in place to cause her father to be born, etc., etc. Every event in Sarah's history in objective time was once a moment of experience in personal time. How could one action at the end of this sequence of physical events have the "metaphysical juice" of existential erasure? Could a time traveler actually be going back to *that time* at which her grandfather lived—backtracking in metaphysically real time? Is this really possible? This is another way of asking whether or not Lewis has fully explored all that it means for time travel to be possible by establishing the personal and objective distinctions in time. Fatalism may be a cheap trick, as Lewis holds, yet time travel cannot be so expensive that a single event in personal time can, in principle, erase those that constituted it in objective time. Lewis seems to have potentially reduplicated a version of the Ability Criticism in attempting to defend a way to hold that time travel is possible. David Foster Wallace's account of situational physical modality and the semantics he provides for it, System J, prove useful for exploring Lewis's account of the shift of context driving the Grandfather Paradox while pushing further into matters of modality.

WALLACE'S SYSTEM J

In "Richard Taylor's 'Fatalism' and the Semantics of Physical Modality," David Foster Wallace further sharpens and elucidates the distinctions with respect to the senses of "can" that Taylor had made in his assessment of the Ability Criticism. Where Taylor distinguished between (logical) possibility, ability, and an action being "within one's power," Wallace distinguishes alethic (logical), physical modality and then, in a crucial move, also distinguishes a type of physical modality, which he terms "situational physical modality" (SPM). This latter modality is so crucial because Wallace determines that it is the level of modality that is at stake when considering the status of future contingent statements. Considering the classic example employed by Taylor of the admiral giving an order (O) today that causes a sea battle (B) tomorrow, Wallace observes:

> The kinds of modalities we are concerned with in an analysis of the Taylor problem must be regarded as situational physical modalities. The alleged entailment-relation between O and B is not logical, and there is no contradiction in (O ∧ ~B). And O does not physically ensure B simpliciter; rather it does so because of, in Taylor's own words, "the totality of other conditions prevailing," and because of the stipulated causal efficacy of O with respect to B *in the situation characterized.*[9]

The extent to which we might be willing to accept Wallace's critique of Taylor's fatalist argument and the semantic system he proposes hinges on whether we accept this distinction in types of physical modalities—"a difference," as he states, "between what is just physically possible in general and what is physically possible for a given agent to do in a given set of circumstances."[10] Physical possibility simpliciter concerns the laws of nature; situational physical modality "concerns the modal character of events, actions, and states of affairs, taking into account not only general and unchanging physical laws, but also the situations and circumstances that can affect what is possible and necessary at certain places at certain times."[11] Importantly, SPM influences any reading of premise five of Taylor's fatalist argument (we presuppose that no agent *can* perform any given act if there is lacking, at the same or any other time, some condition necessary for the occurrence of that act). If Taylor's fatalist conclusion (all actions and inactions are necessary) involves a different sort of modality than that operating in premise five, his argument is rendered invalid. Wallace takes inspiration from the critical literature in developing his position, particularly the Ability Criticism that Taylor had addressed. However, Wallace is well aware that he needs to steer clear of ideas regarding internal skills/ability and must address the *external circumstantial* constraints that premise five concerns.[12] Lewis's notion that a time traveler *can* act in personal time with respect to a narrower context of relevant *facts* (hence can kill her grandfather) amounts to Wallace's understanding of SPM. According to Lewis, the fatalist ushers in irrelevant future facts through shifting context from SPM to a different, broader range of facts (those perceived from the standpoint of objective time). Wallace shows how this problematic shift in context operates semantically.

A key piece of Wallace's semantic machinery, System J, is the application of temporal indexes to situational physical modal statements governed by the (novel) SPM operators he introduces. Situations are joined in "mother-and-daughter" relations that compose causal paths. Mother situations give rise to a (limited) set of possible daughter situations. Daughter situations become, in turn, mothers of another temporally distinct set of daughters, and so on. This model permits a fine-grained tracking of situational physical modalities and, ultimately, their relationships over time, preventing the crucial scope errors that the fatalist argument trades upon. He describes this scope precision:

> Remember that situational physical modalities (the truth-values of physical-modal propositions) vary with time and with the physical situations that obtain at different times. Therefore

the evaluation of any physical modal statement is going to be an evaluation relative to a time and to the physical situation obtaining at that time. Thus we may say that any physical-modal operator in a really well-formed physical-modal formula should appear within the scope of, and be evaluated in the context designated by, a tense-operator or time-marker specifying some time-situation index. When no tense-/time-operator appears to govern a physical-modal operator in a well-formed proposition, the relevant time-and-situation index of evaluation should be understood as an implicit "now."[13]

So, to help clarify, Wallace's system allows us to see that given the absence of a sea battle (~B) *today* (now), we can conclude that it was not possible that the admiral gave his order *yesterday*, but we are not entitled to conclude that *yesterday* the admiral could not give the order. The possibility or impossibility of his giving the order depends on its mother conditions the day before yesterday.

With this disambiguation, however, we also find the most radical feature of System J, a feature Wallace embraces and defends— it allows for *no alternative presents in the context of a given actual present*. Two truths are compossible in System J:

(c) Yesterday it was possible for the admiral to issue order O.
and
(d) It is not possible today that the admiral did issue order O yesterday.[14]

Is this a bug or a feature of his system? Has Wallace inadvertently built a case for fatalism through constructing the machinery to dismantle it? Wallace believes it is a feature—and that System J does not, in the end, justify fatalism. Our unease about how alternative presents are treated in System J is a residual effect of conflating logical and physical possibility. Alternative pasts and alternative futures that are physically compatible with an actual present are permitted in System J, but nevertheless "there are here really no 'alternative presents,' no 'worlds' contemporary with the actual world now, and with at least one feature different from the features of the situation that obtains in the actual world now, which are nevertheless physically *compatible* with the situation that obtains in the actual world now."[15] Wallace emphasizes that his conception of SPM differs from Kripke/Montague models of modality, which are not contextually and temporally sensitive. His diagnosis is compelling:

> These philosophers understand possibility as a *synchronic* relation between cotemporal, ideally existing worlds. They think of "alternative presents" in terms of an infinitely long row of alternative logically possible worlds intersecting a horizontal time-axis at "now." They think of evaluating "present possibilities" in terms of ranging along that row of simultaneous worlds, rather as one might scan a shopping list. When they feel they are being denied any alternative presents, these philosophers may be inclined to see their row of worlds suddenly collapsing into a single constraining actuality-turned-necessity.[16]

Since System J models only physical situational possibility contextually, it does not deny that there are alternative *logically* possible presents. For Wallace, System J accurately reflects common sense regarding the actual physical present: "What is actual now is, quite obviously, physically compatible with what was actual a few moments ago and gave rise to what is actual now."[17] Moreover, given this fixity of actual physical presents once they are actualized, System J preserves fatalism about the past—a result that Taylor himself would find amenable.

SYSTEM J AND TIME TRAVEL

Returning to Lewis's treatment of the Grandfather Paradox with System J at hand, the activities of a time traveler can be reexamined. It starts to look as though time travel itself is a kind of thought experiment that is so much the worse off if, as Lewis insists, we decide that the time traveler *can* kill her grandfather (or even herself at an earlier age), in what Lewis finds to be the narrow sense of personal time regarding situational, local facts. Under System J, there simply is no way a time traveler can actually and physically return to a past moment in personal time. There is nothing in System J that blocks the *conceivability* of this. Yet, to conceive of this possibility, for Wallace, cannot be confused with what is physically and actually possible. Returning again to Lewis's diagnosis, if we decide to consider the time traveler given the broadest range of relevant facts via objective time, the time traveler cannot kill her own grandfather. The logical contradiction involved operates in this context. Our conceptions of time travel— the stories we create—have coherence because it is easy enough to focus on the personal time of a time traveler to spin a familiar narrative about what characters can do. The fascinating loops in time that emerge in such narratives gain effectiveness from the logical contradictions that accrue to the time traveler and whatever she does in objective time.

It is difficult to say whether or not Wallace would consider of the fictionalization of time travel to the past resulting from his position on fatalism to be a bug or a feature of his system. On the one hand, strongly preserving free will through solving Taylor's fatalist problem motivated Wallace's construction of System J. On the other hand, Wallace's construction of a metaphysical argument aimed at showing that Taylor's semantic argument cannot lead to metaphysical conclusions comes at a metaphysical price. Present physical actuality, privileged by System J, is sharply distinguished from logical possibility and, as we have seen in the case of time travel, conceivability. An author of fiction might hesitate to sever fictional realms from the actual physical world so cleanly and decisively. Then again, perhaps not. The elegance involved in dismantling two mirrored counterintuitive positions about what we can and cannot do in the future and the past could prove the most irresistible feature of System J.

NOTES

1. Richard Taylor, "Fatalism," *Philosophical Review* 71, no. 1 (January 1962): 58. Emphasis mine. Also in *David Foster Wallace: Fate, Time, and Language— An Essay on Free Will*, ed. S. Cahn and M. Eckert (New York: Columbia University Press, 2010), 43.
2. Richard Taylor, "A Note on Fatalism," *Philosophical Review* 72, no. 4 (October 1963): 99. Also in *David Foster Wallace: Fate, Time, and Language— An Essay on Free Will*, ed. S. Cahn and M. Eckert (New York: Columbia University Press, 2010), 87–88.
3. Taylor, "Fatalism," 56; also in *David Foster Wallace: Fate, Time, and Language*, 41–42.
4. David Lewis, "The Paradoxes of Time Travel," *American Philosophical Quarterly* (April 1976): 145–152.
5. Ibid., 149.
6. Ibid., 151.
7. Ibid.
8. Ibid., 152.
9. David Foster Wallace, "Richard Taylor's 'Fatalism' and the Semantics of Physical Modality," in *Fate, Time, and Language: An Essay on Free Will*, by David Foster Wallace, ed. S. Cahn and M. Eckert (New York: Columbia University Press, 2010), 150.
10. Ibid., 148.
11. Ibid.
12. Ibid., 152. Wallace covers Taylor's response to Bruce Aune and the Ability Criticism in this section of his thesis. He states here: "Just what Taylor means by 'circumstantial constraint' may become clearer in the context of a related objection to presupposition 5 advanced by Bruce Aune. How proper is it to say that I 'cannot,' have not the ability to, perform an act

if I am absent a condition necessary for that act? For instance, it is often a necessary condition of my doing p that I *try* to do p, but do we say that in those cases when I do not try to do p it follows that I lack the power or ability to do p? In order for me to play tennis, it is necessary that I have a tennis racket, but does the absence of a racket mean that I lack the ability to play tennis? Quite clearly not. But Taylor and others have reasonably replied that the 'cannot' of the Taylor problem is a 'cannot' of circumstances, not really of ability, that it represents an exterior, not an interior, limitation."

13. Ibid., 172.
14. Ibid., 193.
15. Ibid.
16. Ibid., 197.
17. Ibid.

5

DAVID FOSTER WALLACE
AS AMERICAN HEDGEHOG

DANIEL R. KELLY

The fox knows many things; the hedgehog knows one big thing.

—ARCHILOCHUS, EIGHTH CENTURY BC

So was David Foster Wallace a fox or a hedgehog? There isn't an obvious answer to the question. Clearly he knew a great many things, ranging from postmodern literary theory to the history and development of the mathematical concept of infinity, and from the paradoxical effectiveness of the simple clichés of Alcoholics Anonymous to the arcana of the U.S. tax code. On the other hand, despite the sometimes overwhelming breadth of what he knew about, the more familiar one becomes with Wallace's body of work the more difficult it is to escape the feeling that there is something distinctively hedgehog-ish about it. But if he was a hedgehog, what was the one big thing that he knew?

This isn't an easy question to answer either, but there are a number of recognizable and interrelated themes that recur throughout his body of work. These themes—language and meaning; choice and the will; the self, selfishness, solipsism, and their prospects for being overcome—all emanate from a core concern with, roughly, what it means "to be a real human being" (McCaffery 1993). This concern and many of the themes he used to explore it were present right from the beginning, manifest in different ways in each of his two undergraduate senior theses (Wallace 1987, 2010; see also Ryerson 2010). Some of the contradictory impulses found in his corpus were there from the beginning as well. His life's work bespeaks a faith in the importance and power of language. By his own reckoning he thought it could be used to apply "CPR to those elements of what's human and magical that still live and glow" (McCaffery 1993). He was on the Usage Panel for the fourth edition of the *American Heritage Dictionary of the English Language*, a self-described SNOOT[1] whose attention to the details of proper grammar and vocabulary was beyond meticulous, someone so preternaturally adept and inventive with words that a contemporary measured the effect of his death by stating that "the language is impoverished" (Sullivan 2011). Wallace ended up devoting his life to writing, using language to map out and make vivid the current state of the human condition, but he also harbored doubts about his instrument, or at least deep suspicions about some of its common uses. Doubts of this sort inform one of the core concerns of his undergraduate thesis in philosophy. The method of "Richard Taylor's 'Fatalism' and the Semantics of Physical Modality" is to delve into the logical structure of a family of highly nuanced locutions about time and possibility, ultimately to show that Taylor's substantive fatalist conclusion does not follow from his merely linguistic premises: "if Taylor and the fatalists want to force upon us a metaphysical conclusion, they must do metaphysics, *not* semantics. And this seems entirely appropriate" (Wallace 2010, 213).

The larger motivation for that paper, however, centers not so much on language but on another of the themes that would dominate Wallace's career. The aim of the thesis is to rebut Taylor's conclusion and so to undermine its apparent foreclosure on the very possibility of free will. Wallace's own conclusion is modest and purely negative; he wants only to refute an argument that attempts to show choice is impossible. He does not mount a positive case that free will is, indeed, possible (let alone actual), nor does he attempt to capture the essence of genuine choice, or to say how an individual might fail or succeed to express her free will, or how in succeeding she might choose well or poorly. But he never abandons those topics. While Wallace eventually opted for the tools of the writer of novels, short stories, literary journalism, and narrative nonfiction rather than those of the logician and analytic philosopher, he continued to use language to explore the themes of choice and free will from a remarkable number of angles over the course of his lifetime.[2] Those who feel drawn to the view that there is something distinctively hedgehog-ish about Wallace might also be tempted to think that the "one big thing" he knew had something to do with the challenges and pitfalls of choosing, and the ways in which problems connected to choice presented themselves to those of us living in the turn-of-the-millennium United States. Since I am both so drawn and so tempted, this is the case I will make in this essay. Much of it will be devoted to identifying, fleshing out, and presenting in a linear manner what I see as one of, if not the, major lines of thought about choice and free will that weaves its way through the Wallace oeuvre and the main images and metaphors he used to express it.

GIVING YOURSELF AWAY

In their recent book *All Things Shining*, the philosophers Hubert Dreyfus and Sean Kelly begin with the idea that our culture is currently in the grip of a predicament that is not merely moral but deeply existential, and perhaps distinctive of our moment in history: "in the contemporary world we face a deeper and more difficult problem. It is not just that we know the course of right action and fail to pursue it; we often seem not to have any sense for what the standards of living a good life are in the first place. Or said another way, we seem to have no ground for choosing one course of action over any other" (2011, 15).

As they continue to articulate and explore this predicament, they use the details of Wallace's work, life, and death as way to bring out what they call "the burden of choice." In its most general form,

> The burden of choice, as we have called it . . . amounts to profound questions: how, given the kinds of being that we are, is it possible to live a *meaningful* life? Or more particularly, where are we to find the significant differences among the possible actions in our lives? For it is these differences that provide a basis for making decisions about who we are to be or become. . . . All of these questions ultimately seem to lead them back to the basic one: On what basis should I make this choice?
>
> (2011, 12)

Dreyfus and Kelly use Wallace to motivate their discussion because they see him as being especially sensitive to the toll the burden of choice can take, and believe that he had a gift for revealing the ways in which it imposes itself on contemporary individuals and the measures people might take in dealing with it—or trying to avoid it. They are impressed with the fact that he wrestled with the problem on a personal level as well. For them, Wallace was "the proverbial canary in the coal mine of modern existence" (2011, 26).[3]

Wallace does tackle this very problem, and in doing so he uses a number of approaches to recast it in fresh and illuminating ways. One phrase that turns up in a number of different places is the "need to give yourself away," which Wallace uses to talk about an inner drive that he seems confident most of his readers will recognize in one form or another. For instance, Hal Incandenza, one of the protagonists of *Infinite Jest* and an adolescent prodigy who has spent most of his life at a top tennis academy, notes that "experience seems to suggest that people are virtually unlimited in their need to give themselves away, on various levels" (Wallace 1996, 53). He later reflects on the insight, but with much more ambivalence:

It now lately sometimes seemed like a kind of black miracle to me that people could actually care deeply about a subject or pursuit, and could go on caring this way for years on end. Could dedicate their entire lives to it. It seemed admirable and at the same time pathetic. We are dying to give ourselves away to something, maybe. God or Satan, politics or grammar, topology or philately—the object seemed incidental to this will to give oneself away, utterly. To games or needles, to some other person. Something pathetic about it. A flight-from in the form of a plunging-into. Flight from what, exactly? . . . To what purpose? This was why they started us so young [at the tennis academy]: to give ourselves away before the age when the questions *why* and *to what* grow real beaks and claws. It was kind, in a way.

(900)

Wallace himself uses the same expression while talking to David Lipsky about his motivation in writing *Infinite Jest*: "The book isn't supposed to be about *drugs*, getting off drugs. Except as the fact that drugs are kind of a metaphor for the sort of addictive continuum that I think has to do with how we as a culture relate to things that are alive. . . . So I think it's got something to do with, that we're just—we're absolutely dying to give ourselves away to something" (Lipsky 2008, 81). Wallace goes on:

I wanted to do something that was very, very much about America. And the things that ended up for me being most distinctively *American* right now, around the millennium, had to do with both

entertainment and about some kind of weird, addictive um . . .
wanting to give yourself away to something. That I ended up
thinking was kind of a distorted religious impulse. And a lot
of the AA stuff in the book was mostly an excuse, was to try to
have—it's very hard to talk about people's relationship with any
kind of God, in any book later than like Dostoyevsky. I mean the
culture, it's all wrong for it.

(LIPSKY 2008, 82)[4]

There are two ideas in these passages that I want to flesh out.
The first has to do with the anatomy of the picture Wallace briefly
sketches; the second with the hazards of choice presented by turn-
of-the-millennium America.

CHOOSING A TEMPLE

Much of what Wallace says about choice and the need to give
yourself away can be fit into a schema made of three distinct,
general components: (1) the primal *need* or basic *impulse* to give
away or invest, (2) a sort of *resource* that is "given away" or type
of *currency* that a person is driven to invest, and (3) the objects
at which the impulse might be directed, the *vessels* with which
the resource might be filled, into which the currency might be
channeled. Choice and its many burdens enter the picture at the
third step, when a person must decide between a range of options
about where to direct his impulse, what to invest in. The specifics
of individual manifestations and particular cases obviously dif-
fer, but this general schema of components can be used to reveal
some telling commonalities in how Wallace often dramatizes the
problem and addresses his questions and concerns about choice.
Among these concerns is a desire to better grasp the interplay
between the first two components and the third component, to

scrutinize, understand, and peek behind the strange blind spot that the narrator of *Infinite Jest* describes in Hal and his contemporaries: "Like most North Americans of his generation, Hal tends to know way less about why he feels certain ways about the objects and pursuits he's devoted to than he does about the objects and pursuits themselves" (Wallace 1996, 54).

In identifying the first component as a "need" and an "impulse," Wallace seems to conceive of this part of the phenomena as originating inside the individual, "real human beings" that are driven by it. The impulse is simply there—a deep, inner, human given—and it demands to be satisfied, to be directed somewhere or other. Wallace also appears to see the second component of this picture as a human given, but of the three it is the most difficult to pin down. Wallace talks about the "self" that is given away in the above passages, but the term seems to function as an extremely general catch-all, and an unfortunately ambiguous one. For instance, in "Laughing with Kafka," Wallace (1998) appears to endorse the idea that a self is not, like the impulse or the resource, a given but rather something that each individual human must, over the course of a lifetime, painstakingly *construct*. He bemoans the fact that his undergraduates don't get this, and so don't get Kafka. Rather, they have been mislead by American culture to think "that a self is something you just have." Much of Kafka's humor and appeal remains opaque to them because it lies in his depiction of "the horrific struggle to establish a human self."

Elsewhere Wallace gets more specific. In reflecting on Dostoevsky and religion, Wallace frames the resource and the impulse to invest it in terms of *faith*: "is somehow *needing* to have faith a sufficient reason for having faith? But then what kind of need are we talking about?" (2005, 260). Further along in the same essay he talks about this kind of spendable currency in terms of "passion, conviction, and engagement" (271). In his later work, especially *The Pale King* and the Kenyon address, he discusses the microeconomics of the resource in terms of simple *attention*, to "how and what you think . . . what you pay attention to" (2009). At a more macro level, the resource might be understood as a person's time, what she does with the finite span of her lifetime. At a more abstract level, the currency might be thought of as the kind of significance that, when it is bestowed upon something, gives it personal *meaning*. Using a turn of phrase whose religious connotations he obviously welcomes, Wallace tells his Kenyon audience that what an individual chooses most to invest with meaning and significance, what she devotes her attention and life to, she *worships*.

The term "worship" is used repeatedly and in a similar way throughout a long conversation that takes place in *Infinite Jest* between the Canadian secret operative Remy Marathe and his fellow operative Hugh Steeply. Continuing with the religious imagery, Marathe also uses the term "temple" for the third component of the tripartite schema that I'm using, that is, for whatever it is that is worshipped, whatever vessel a person lavishes attention on, invests passion and sentiment in, devotes her life to: "Our attachments are our temple, what we worship, no? What we give ourselves to, what we invest with faith" (Wallace 1996, 107). Nowadays, different people worship at different temples, devote their lives to different things, of course: drugs, sport, religion, academic excellence, family life, sexual conquest, political causes, various forms of professional achievement, and the hedonistic pursuit of brute pleasure. In his fiction, Wallace imagines what it is like to have made different choices, to worship at one of these temples or another, what the benefits and drawbacks of each might be.[5] But, bringing us back to the issue of free will and the burden of choice, a major part of Wallace's message is that deciding where to direct the resource is as fundamental as decisions get, and that confronting this choice is, for us turn-of-the-millennium Americans, unavoidable. As Marathe puts it, "For this choice determines all else. No? All other of our you say *free* choices follow from this: what is our temple?" (107). Each individual must choose where to aim her own impulse, choose how to invest the currency of her attention and passion, choose how to spend her time and establish her identity, choose what to do with her life. Wallace makes essentially this point in the Kenyon address, where he also expresses it in religious terms, even though the context and emphasis is somewhat different: "Because here's something else that's weird but true: in the day-to-day trenches of adult life, there is actually no such thing as atheism. There is no such thing as not worshipping. Everybody worships. The only choice we get is what to worship" (Wallace 2009).

TOTAL NOISE, CONGENITAL SKEPTICISM, AND THE CAGE

Understood using the more expansive sense of "worship," this last statement threatens to become trivial, but this brings me to the second idea that I want to flesh out, this one about the texture of our moment in history. Wallace was convinced that contemporary America does not do a particularly good job dealing with this impulse and the choices it forces upon us. Much of his work can be understood as exploring *why* and *how* it's so difficult for us to choose well or to even appreciate this whole cluster of issues, and as charting out the ways American culture fails to equip its people to handle those issues, talk about them with one another, or even think clearly about them on their own. He identifies many difficulties, but I'll note three of what I think are the most interesting.

The first factor that makes decision difficult in contemporary America, according to Wallace, is that the number of options and amount of information we have to deal with is overwhelming, and competition for our very attention is enormous. He tells Lipsky

(2010, 17) that "life seems to strobe on and off for me, to barrage me with input," and he puts a slightly different spin on the point in an interview with Laura Miller (1996): "The world that I live in consists of 250 advertisements a day and any number of unbelievably entertaining options, most of which are subsidized by corporations that want to sell me things." This description touches on the calculated seductiveness of advertising ("pay attention to me! buy this!"), but the difficulty I want to bring out is largely epistemic. The flux of contemporary America is endlessly distracting and puts us in a near constant state of information overload. Wallace uses a discussion of the complexities involved in sorting through and choosing something as seemingly simple—or at least as well circumscribed—as the best American essays of 2007 as a jumping-off point for some much larger-scale reflections about the

> Total Noise that's also the sound of our U.S. culture right now, a culture and volume of info and spin and rhetoric and context that I know I'm not alone in finding too much to even absorb, much less to try to make sense of or organize into any kind of triage of saliency or value. Such basic absorption, organization, and triage used to be what was required of an educated adult, a.k.a. an informed citizen—at least that's what I got taught. Suffice it here to say that the requirements now seem different.
>
> (WALLACE 2007, 1–2)

No single mind can encompass the culture, and no individual can consider, let alone absorb and properly evaluate, every claim, position, option, or demand. To get a handle on or even make sense of the flood of information, we are forced to select and rely more and more on what Wallace dubs "Deciders," evaluative filters that we trust to assess, filter, and winnow what is worthy of our full attention.[6] He suggests that we are just beginning to awaken to how this is transforming our abilities to make any decision, only now

starting to become more aware of just how much subcontracting and outsourcing and submitting to other Deciders we're all now forced to do, which is threatening (the inchoate awareness is) to our sense of ourselves as intelligent free agents. And yet there is no clear alternative to this outsourcing and submission. It may possibly be that acuity and taste in choosing which Deciders one submits to is now the real measure of informed adulthood.

(WALLACE 2007, 3)

On this score Wallace gives an expression and diagnosis of his own discomfort with the evolving situation and the resulting fact that we are now forced to choose our own collection of trusted evaluative filters, to essentially decide on a set of Deciders. He did not seem to have any advice on what to do about it, though.

A second aspect of contemporary American culture that Wallace thought aggravates our ability to appreciate and deal with the burden of choice is a certain anathema to unguarded conviction, to simple devotion itself.[7] This puts us in an intolerable dilemma: on the one hand, simply in virtue of being alive and human we are saddled with a kind of existential currency and an unavoidable impulse to invest it in something. On the other hand, as educated, well-off, turn-of-the-millennium Americans we find ourselves instilled with a deep suspicion of both. Wallace throws this feature of our culture into relief by holding up Dostoevsky, whom he deeply admires for appearing "to possess degrees of passion, conviction, and engagement with deep moral issues that we—here, today—cannot or do not permit ourselves" (271). Wallace continues to flesh out his characterization of this aspect of our culture: "there are certain tendencies we believe are bad, qualities we hate and fear. Among them are sentimentality, naïveté, archaism, fanaticism. It would probably be better to call our own art's culture now one of congenital skepticism. Our intelligentsia distrust strong belief, open conviction. Material passion is one thing, but ideological passion disgusts us on some deep level" (Wallace 2005, 272).

Connecting this to the "distorted religious impulse" mentioned earlier, the suggestion here seems to be that this American anathema toward sentiment and conviction is part of what "distorts" the impulse to invest or even express it too deeply. This skepticism has the effect of smothering that core human urge, making it hard for a person to be consciously, proudly, passionately, and unironically devoted to anything—or anything other than perhaps the pursuit of material ends and a life that involves "as little pain and as much pleasure as possible" (Wallace 2005, 261). But for all that, the skepticism and the reticence that comes with it don't make the impulse shut down or disappear. Instead we are left without any outlet, frustrated and stifled until we end up "dying to give ourselves away to something."

In his essay "E Unibus Pluram: Television and U.S. Fiction," Wallace traces out in great detail how this congenital skepticism is related to irony and ironic distancing, and how both have come to dominate television, and in turn himself and his generation of American fiction writers. While charting out another manifestation of this aspect of the distinctively American difficulties with choice and devotion, he offers a bit of guidance, at least to the next generation of artists: "The next real literary 'rebels' in this country might . . . have the childish gall actually to endorse and instantiate single-entendre principles. Who treat of plain old untrendy human troubles and emotions in U.S. life with reverence and conviction. . . . To risk accusations of sentimentality, melodrama" (1997, 81).

It is not immediately clear what advice to extract from this for someone struggling with the burden of choice and the best way to create a meaningful life, rather than an artist struggling to create meaningful art. Perhaps, connecting it to the claim that the impulse cannot simply be shut down, making the decision of where to direct it unavoidable, the suggestion in this quote can be interpreted as urging us to better appreciate the abstract and difficult-to-grasp contours of the intolerable dilemma in which our American moment places us. In effect, it is a call for the kind of clarity that is better achieved through sincerity and direct honesty rather than mockery or coded irony. Since, as he puts it elsewhere, "everybody worships," getting clearer about this fact might also help us get more comfortable with it, and so be less disposed to the kind of knee-jerk suspicion toward passionate engagement or deep conviction that Wallace sees as distinctive of our current, congenitally skeptical outlook.

Indeed, this brings us to a third source of difficulty, one that can be found in passages where Wallace suggests there is something about contemporary America that corrodes its people's capacity for choice itself. Wallace often expresses this strand of thought in terms of hedonism and addiction. For instance, he takes up the familiar idea that American culture is adolescent, but pushes it further, claiming we live in a culture that is not just adolescent, but hedonistic and selfish. He goes on to note that in its most extreme, undiluted form, the package of adolescence, hedonism, and selfishness can easily lead to addiction. Wallace makes the point about adolescence in a footnote (and a footnote to that footnote) in "Laughing with Kafka" where he says

a crude but concise way to put the whole thing is that our present culture is, both developmentally and historically, "adolescent." . . . The single most stressful and frightening period of human development—the stage when the adulthood we claim to crave begins to present itself as a real and narrowing system of responsibilities and limitations.

A common response of adolescents to this stress and fright is to indulge their most hardcore hedonistic tendencies and "do their most serious falling-down drinking and drugging and reckless driving and rampant fucking and mindless general Dionysian-type reveling" (Wallace 1998, nn2, 2a).

As noted above, Wallace develops the connection to addiction explicit in his conversation with David Lipsky (2010), and it is one of the major themes of *Infinite Jest*. Some of the book's most memorable images depict the effect that complete addiction can have on an addict's will, distorted impulse, and capacity for choice, and they are peppered throughout the novel. One of the most recurrent image is that of *the cage*. The metaphor is used to illustrate how an addictive Substance, say a drug that initially seems to offer an instant kind of freedom—an escape from the self and the burden of choice—slowly and insidiously creates a need so dire and encompassing that it swamps out everything else, all other choices, leaving the addict trapped in a choice-nullifying prison that seems inescapable. Another family of images, usually offered by and to recovering addicts, tends to be insectoid: "the chilling Hispanic term for whatever interior disorder drives the addict back again and again to the enslaving Substance is *tecato gusano*, which apparently connotes some kind of interior psychic worm that cannot be sated or killed" (Wallace 1996, 200). And also:

> Eugenio Martinez over at Ennet House never tires of pointing out that your personal will is the web your Disease sits and spins in, still. The will you call your own ceased to be yours as of who knows how many Substance-drenched years ago. It's now shot through with the spidered fibrosis of your Disease. His own experience's term for the Disease is: *The Spider*. You have to Starve The Spider: you have to surrender your will.

(357)

Something about American culture, the suggestion seems to be, encourages this kind of flight from the pressures of choice. But of course choice is inescapable, and the easy, seductive, hedonistic alternatives, as tempting as they might initially seem, lead to an even less bearable situation: a gradual enslavement, where the eventual addict becomes ensnared by a "temple" she initially, though unwisely and unreflectively, freely choose.

Complaints about shortcomings of this sort are made by many of the non-American characters throughout the novel. Marathe makes the case that Americans are unable to exercise control or critical judgment over "what we give ourselves to, what we invest with faith" (1996, 107), claiming that "someone sometime let you forget how to choose, and what. Someone let your people forget it was the only thing of importance, choosing" (Wallace 1996, 319). Wallace also portrays Gerhard Schtitt, the old-school German and director of the tennis academy, as slightly horrified by (the novel's fictionalized version of) contemporary America, finding it "hilarious and frightening at the same time." He sees the country as at least tacitly encouraging its citizens to mindlessly devote themselves to nothing more than a "sloppy intersection of desires and fears" and the "primacy of straight-line pursuing this flat and short-sighted idea of personal happiness" (Wallace 1996, 82).

Schtitt is able to acknowledge that this is a recipe for happiness of a certain, shallow sort, but he is more impressed by its inevitable and toxic byproduct of loneliness: "The happy pleasure of the person alone, yes? . . . Lonely" (Wallace 1996, 82). Wallace sounds a similar note in his Kenyon address, when he warns graduating seniors that the contemporary American adult world they are about to enter "hums merrily along in a pool of fear and anger and frustration and craving and worship of self. Our own present culture has harnessed these forces in ways that have yielded extraordinary wealth and comfort and personal freedom. The freedom all to be lords of our tiny skull-sized kingdoms, alone at the center of all creation" (2009). He also points out that this world does "not discourage you from operating on your default settings" of adolescent self-centeredness and that the Total Noise of contemporary America that invites us to remain in those default settings can seduce us into forgetting that organizing a life around this kind of lonely freedom and hedonistic pursuit of pleasure is even a choice at all, and not the one we have to make.

Wallace's most fundamental piece of positive advice on this, I think, can be distilled down to two simple words: *wake up*. The reason his Kenyon address feels like a skeleton key to his entire body of work is that it makes this point not obliquely or as the implicit moral of a story, but directly, with all of the "rhetorical niceties stripped away" (Wallace 2009). In under four thousands words, he sounds a clarion call to pay more and better attention to choosing—choosing where you direct your energy and core human impulse, choosing where to invest your passion, your conviction, your time, even choosing something as seemingly mundane as what to pay attention to on a day-to-day, hour-by-hour, minute-by-minute basis. More than that, though, he is at pains to drive home the point that these are, in fact, *choices*, they are opportunities to exercise free will, and they remain ubiquitous. Part of his message is that this is shockingly easy to miss or forget: "If your total freedom of choice regarding what to think about seems too obvious to waste time discussing, I'd ask you to think about fish and water, and to bracket for just a few minutes your skepticism about the value of the totally obvious" (Wallace 2009).[8] If the problem is that contemporary American culture corrodes its people's capacity for choice by distracting them, or by leaving them ill equipped to recognize opportunities to choose, or by actively discouraging individuals from "choosing to do the work of somehow altering or getting free of [their] natural, hard-wired default setting" (Wallace 2009), then Wallace's solution is, in effect, expressed throughout his body of work itself. Again and again, in story after story and article after article, he tries to wake his readers up, to make them see, make them more awake, alert, and aware of the contemporary American water, of how it affects those of us swimming through it, of the possibilities for choice and action that it affords us, but that we might have missed.

IT'S CALLED FREE WILL, SHERLOCK

David Foster Wallace was a champion of choice and a student of the problems associated with agency and free will throughout his entire life. For most of it, he did not address "the" problem of free will as it is typically presented in an introduction to philosophy course, or as it is framed in the philosophical literature on fatalism to which his undergraduate philosophy thesis was a contribution. But the case that I've been making here is that at the heart of Wallace's work is a concern with choice that animates and informs nearly his entire corpus, from beginning to tragically early end. It was his big thing, the lens through which he viewed and made sense of the American world around him, the one subject by which he was most exercised and about which he had the most to say.

I'll end by noting that there is another, perhaps equally visible, line of thought that runs throughout Wallace's work and that centers on difficulties raised by self-consciousness about fraudulence and authenticity, performance and genuineness, and the seemingly inescapable double-binds that too much self-awareness can land one in. This strand is present but more peripheral in *Infinite Jest*; it is near the center of many of the stories in *Brief Interviews with Hideous Men*, especially "Octet" (Wallace 2000, 111–136); in *The Pale King* it is most near the surface and presented with an interesting twist in the long conversation between Meredith Rand and Shane Drinion (Wallace 2011, 446–511); and it finds its best and fullest expression in what one commentator called Wallace's "last great story" (Baskin 2009), "Good Old Neon" (Wallace 2004, 141–181). The reason I bring it up here is that it might seem to undermine my main thesis, namely that Wallace was a hedgehog and that the unifying theme of his work is a concern with choice.

For now, I can only point to where a response to this challenge might begin. On the one hand, it is not at all obvious that the "fraudulence paradox" is fundamentally about choice or free will. Neal, the main character of "Good Old Neon," certainly doesn't describe it in those terms:

> The fraudulence paradox was that the more time and effort you put into trying to appear impressive or attractive to other people, the less impressive or attractive you felt inside—you were a fraud. And the more of a fraud you felt like, the harder you tried to convey an impressive or likable image of yourself so that other people wouldn't find out what a hollow, fraudulent person you really were.
>
> (WALLACE 2004, 147)

On the other hand, part of the greatness of this particular story is that Wallace doesn't rest content merely describing that paradox or its accompanying labyrinths of in-bent self-consciousness or simply illustrating the psychological havoc these kinds of double-binds can wreak on those caught in their grip (c.f. "The Depressed Person," Wallace 2000, 31–58). Rather, he goes on to offer words of reassurance, and he even sneaks in some salutary advice about how to dissolve the problem and escape the double-bind. That intriguing, if murky, piece of advice explicitly connects these two major lines of thought in Wallace's work: "You think it makes you a fraud, the tiny fraction anyone else ever sees? Of course you're a fraud, of course what people see is never you. And of course you know this, and of course you try to manage what part they see if you know it's only a part. Who wouldn't? It's called free will, Sherlock" (Wallace 2004, 179).

I do not, alas, have the space to map out the cluster of ideas, metaphors, and images Wallace uses to explore self-consciousness and the fraudulence paradox. A promising place to start would be with the observation that the issues surrounding authenticity and fraudulence are deeply related to questions about the nature of the self. As we have seen, on at least one way Wallace often thinks about the self, the process of constructing a self and the question of how to present it best in everyday life seem to be shot through with opportunities for choice, even if we don't always realize it. And such choices, like all choices, can be made well or poorly. In any event, I certainly think that the full project of exploring this theme in Wallace's thought is worthwhile. Of the many fruits that project might bear is a better grasp of the interplay between that theme and the one I have examined here, as well as and a deeper understanding of what, for me, is one of the most perplexing but suggestive sentences in all of his work.

NOTES

I am grateful to Michael Brownstein, Damon Centola, Matt Guschwan, Michael Johnston, Nina Strohminger, Natalia Washington, and an anonymous reviewer for useful feedback on earlier drafts of this paper, and especially to Scott Cherry and Karl Kurtz for comments on the paper and many lengthy, invigorating conversations about Wallace and his work.

1. A term, taken from his childhood, that Wallace uses throughout his essay "Authority and American Usage" to denote "a really extreme usage fanatic" and that was an acronym for either "Sprachgefuhl Necessitate Our Ongoing Tendance" or "Syntax Nudniks of Our Time" (Wallace 2005, 69n5).

2. As we will see, over the course of his career Wallace became less interested in the more metaphysical facets of choice and the traditional dialectic between free will and fatalism, and was instead drawn toward

the more ethical, epistemic, and existential facets, which, perhaps not coincidentally, are also those that bear more directly on the quality of our daily lives. With that in mind, it may be the case that much of what Wallace talks about under the monikers of free will and choice will not interest certain analytic philosophers who understand and use the term "free will" in particular, technical ways.

3. Dreyfus and Kelly also see in Wallace's work a final, specific *recommendation* about the best way to handle the burden of choice: "The sole possibility for meaning, according to Wallace, is found in the strength of the individual's will" (2011, 45), and "the sacred in Wallace—insofar as he can see such a phenomenon at all—is something that *we impose* upon experience; there is nothing *given* about it at all. For Wallace anything—even some type of 'consumer-hell'—can be experienced as sacred if I choose to make it so" (2011, 47).

This is not the place to engage in a full and proper debate about this, so I will briefly state my main objection. In short, I disagree that Dreyfus and Kelly identify a unique or even definitive statement of Wallace's prescriptive ideas on the matter; certainly, he explores many, and he adopts different views in different places, often for different rhetorical purposes. Dreyfus and Kelly tend to focus on his later writing, particularly the Kenyon commencement address (Wallace 2009) and *The Pale King* (Wallace 2011). The view found there, however, is difficult to square with the fact that he also writes often and with apparent approval about *surrendering* the will to something larger than one's self.

4. It is not clear from the context why Wallace thinks the impulse that American culture distorts is "religious." A plausible interpretation, suggested by Dreyfus and Kelly, is that in earlier eras there would be no question, no choice or range of options about where to direct the impulse—it would have been handled by religion: "Although the burden of choice can seem inevitable, in fact it is unique to contemporary life. It is not just that in earlier epochs one knew on what basis one's most fundamental existential choices were made: it is that the existential questions didn't even make sense. Consider the Middle Ages, for example. During this period in the Christian West a person's identity was determined by God. . . . it was virtually inconceivable that one's identity might be determined in any other way" (2011, 13).

Needless to say, our way of life has changed dramatically. Once, the story goes, societies were organized around a single dominant normative framework and so offered only a single kind of path or tightly limited class of vessels, dictated by religious culture so much taken for granted that it was invisible. In today's secular age, however, our culture presents a wide range of options for where to direct the impulse, how to organize our concern, construct our identity, and invest our selves (also see Taylor 1989, 2007). Moreover, our culture's options do not even seem to be fixed, but are obviously malleable, evolving at a faster and arguably accelerating pace. Hence, perhaps, the epigraph to *The Pale King*: "We fill pre-existing forms and when we fill them we change them and are changed.—Frank Bidart."

5. Though I'm not convinced he ever makes a grand or final pronouncement on which "temple" is the best or right one, Wallace certainly doesn't remain completely neutral or reserve all judgment. He maps out the psychological and physical hell that drugs lead to in *Infinite Jest*. He seems of two minds on the issue of devotion to sport, the "temple" that is the focus of the other half of *Infinite Jest*. Elsewhere, he emphasizes some of the positives in "Federer as Religious Experience" (Wallace 2006) while highlighting some of the negatives in "How Tracy Austin Broke My Heart" (in Wallace 2005, 141–155). But I think he is most eloquent about the tradeoffs in "Tennis Player Michael Joyce's Professional Artistry as a Paradigm of Certain Stuff About Choice, Freedom, Discipline, Joy, Grotesquerie, and Human Completeness." About athletes in general, he says: "Bismarck's epigram about diplomacy and sausages applies also to the way we Americans seem to feel about professional athletes. . . . But we prefer not to countenance the kinds of sacrifices the professional-grade athlete has made to get so good at one particular thing. . . . But the actual facts of the sacrifices repel us when we see them: basketball geniuses who cannot read, sprinters who dope themselves, defensive tackles who shoot up bovine hormones until they collapse or explode. We prefer not to consider the shockingly vapid and primitive comments uttered by athletes in postcontest interviews, or to imagine what impoverishments in one's mental life would allow people actually to think in the simplistic way great athletes seem to think . . . the realities of top-level athletics today require an early and total commitment to one pursuit. An almost ascetic focus. A subsumption of almost all other features of human life to their one chosen talent and pursuit. A consent to live in a world that, like a child's world, is very serious and very small" (Wallace 1997, 236–237).

About Michael Joyce himself, Wallace has this to say: "The restrictions on his life have been, in my opinion, grotesque; and in certain ways Joyce himself is grotesque. But the radical compression of his attention and self has allowed him to become a transcendent practitioner of an art—something few of us get to be. It's allowed him to visit and test parts of his psyche that most of us do not even know for sure we have, to manifest in concrete form virtues like courage, persistence in the face of pain or exhaustion, performance under wilting scrutiny and pressure. . . . He is an American and he wants to win. He wants this, and he will pay to have it—will pay just to pursue it, let it define him—and will pay with the regretless cheer of a man for whom issues of choice became irrelevant long ago" (Wallace 1997, 254–255).

In the Kenyon address, he preaches being alert to the opportunities for choice, rather than advocating sport or any other particular temple, though he does warn that "the compelling reason for maybe choosing some sort of god or spiritual-type thing to worship—be it JC or Allah, be it YHWH or the Wiccan Mother Goddess, or the Four Noble Truths, or some inviolable set of ethical principles—is that pretty much anything else you worship will eat you alive" (Wallace 2009).

Overall, though, Wallace seems to have been most tempted by a view similar to that awkwardly expressed in *Infinite Jest* by Gerhard Schtitt, to the effect that it is best to be devoted to anything as long as it is larger than your self, understood here as your own immediate desires, appetites, and pleasures. According to Schtitt, to be devoted to nothing but the self is to be ultimately unhappy on some deep level, alone, and lost: "Without there is something bigger. Nothing to contain and give the meaning. Lonely. *Verstiegenheit.** . . . Any something. The *what*: this is more unimportant than that there is *something*" (Wallace 1996, 83). *"(Low-Bavarian for something like 'wandering alone in blasted disorienting territory beyond all charted limits and orienting markers,' supposedly" (Wallace 1996, 994).

6. See Pariser (2011) for an accessible and thought-provoking investigation of this phenomena and the "filter bubble" it creates around us.

7. This may be to best place to acknowledge that of course there is no single uniform "American culture." Moreover, segments of the contemporary United States welcome and even encourage the kind of straightforward, passionate dedication being discussed here. I take Wallace to be speaking for and to a recognizable segment of the population, namely,

a segment that, well, that would be reading something written by David Foster Wallace.

8. As Dreyfus and Kelly put the point, "Practices that a whole culture takes for granted are extremely difficult to identify" (2011, 17). Wallace begins his Kenyon address with a joke that illustrates exactly this point: "There are these two young fish swimming along and they happen to meet an older fish swimming the other way, who nods at them and says 'Morning, boys. How's the water?' And the two young fish swim on for a bit, and then eventually one of them looks over at the other and goes 'What the hell is water?'" The mention of "fish and water" from the quote in the main text is an allusion to this opening joke.

REFERENCES

Baskin, J. 2009. "Death Is Not The End: David Foster Wallace: His Legacy and Critics." *The Point* 1 (spring).

Dreyfus, H., and S. Kelly. 2011. *All Things Shining: Reading the Western Classics to Find Meaning in a Secular Age*. New York: Free Press.

Lipsky, D. 2010. *Although of Course You End Up Becoming Yourself: A Road Trip with David Foster Wallace*. New York: Broadway.

Max, D. T. 2012. *Every Love Story Is a Ghost Story: A Life of David Foster Wallace*. New York: Viking.

McCaffery, L. 1993. "A Conversation with David Foster Wallace." *Review of Contemporary Fiction* 13, no. 2 (summer).

Pariser, E. 2011. *The Filter Bubble: What the Internet Is Hiding from You*. New York: Penguin.

Ryerson, J. 2010. "Introduction: A Head That Throbbed Heartlike: The Philosophical Mind of David Foster Wallace." In *Fate, Time, and Language: An Essay on Free Will*, by David Foster Wallace, ed. S. Cahn and M. Eckert. New York: Columbia University Press.

Sullivan, J. J. 2011. "Too Much Information." *GQ* (May).

Taylor, C. 1989. *Sources of the Self: The Making of Modern Identity*. Cambridge, MA: Harvard University Press.

Taylor, C. 2007. *The Secular Age*. Cambridge, MA: Harvard University Press.

Wallace, D. F. 1987. *The Broom of the System*. New York: Viking.

——. 1996. *Infinite Jest*. Cambridge: Cambridge University Press.

——. 1997. *A Supposedly Fun Thing I'll Never Do Again: Essays and Arguments*. New York: Little Brown.

——. 1998. "Laughing with Kafka." *Harper's* (July).

——. 2000. *Brief Interviews with Hideous Men.* New York: Back Bay.

——. 2004. *Oblivion: Stories.* New York: Back Bay.

——. 2005. *Consider the Lobster.* New York: Little, Brown.

——. 2006. "Federer as Religious Experience." *New York Times Magazine: Play* (August 20).

——. 2007. "Deciderization 2007—a Special Report." In *The Best American Essays 2007*, ed. D. F. Wallace and R. Atwan. Boston: Mariner.

——. 2009. *This Is Water: Some Thoughts, Delivered on a Significant Occasion, About Living a Compassionate Life.* New York: Little, Brown.

——. 2010. *Fate, Time, and Language: An Essay on Free Will.* Ed. S. Cahn and M. Eckert. New York: Columbia University Press.

——. 2011. *The Pale King.* Cambridge: Cambridge University Press.

DAVID FOSTER WALLACE ON THE GOOD LIFE

NATHAN BALLANTYNE AND JUSTIN TOSI

Dostoevsky wrote fiction about the stuff that's really important. He wrote fiction about identity, moral value, death, will, sexual vs. spiritual love, greed, freedom, obsession, reason, faith, suicide. And he did it without ever reducing his characters to mouthpieces or his books to tracts. His concern was always what it is to be a human being—that is, how to be an actual person, someone whose life is informed by values and principles, instead of just an especially shrewd kind of self-preserving animal.

—DAVID FOSTER WALLACE, "JOSEPH FRANK'S DOSTOEVSKY"

David Foster Wallace thought that the point of writing fiction was to explore what it is to be a human being.[1] In this essay, we argue that his writings suggest a view about what philosophers would call the *good life*. Wallace's perspective is subtle and worthy of attention. We'll contrast what Wallace says with some popular positions from moral philosophy and contemporary culture.

Wallace said much about ethical matters even though he didn't write on them formally or systematically. How then shall we distill views from his writings? Our strategy is to present Wallace's reactions, as found in his fiction and some essays, to three positions about the good life. We will ask what Wallace would make of those positions and thus try to triangulate his own view by reference to them.

The first position we'll explore is sometimes called *ironism*. More often practiced than defended, for reasons that will be evident, ironism involves distancing oneself from everything one says or does and putting on what Wallace often calls a "mask of ennui." Ironism appeals to us, Wallace thought, because it insulates us from criticism, both from others and from ourselves. After all, if someone dismisses what she does as unimportant or even meaningless, she can hardly be criticized for valuing it too much. But such a person can be criticized for failing to value anything, and this is Wallace's response to the ironist. Wallace thinks that our lives should be about *something*. He underlines the value of sincere self-identification with what one does and cares about.

According to a second kind of position, what philosophers call *hedonism*, a good life consists in pleasure. Wallace would reject any form of hedonism, we surmise, because he doubts that pleasure could play such a fundamental role in the good life. A life of enjoyment is a life of private enjoyment, and we mangle values like friendship by explaining their value solely in terms of our pleasure. A good human life involves a richer assortment of goods than these theories capture.

On a third family of views—*narrative theories*, as we'll call them—a good human life is characterized by fidelity to a unified narrative. This is a systematic story about one's life, composed of a set of ends or principles according to which one lives. The story lays down the terms of success for a good life. Failing to live up to the story means failing to flourish. But Wallace's fiction is rife with characters who are unhappy at least partly because they try (and fail) to live up to their stories. Narrative theories, he thinks, turn people into spectators to, rather than participants in, their own lives.

We conclude that Wallace sees serious flaws in these three popular views. But Wallace also suggests an attractive method for pursuing moral questions. Not unlike Wittgenstein, Wallace thought his task was to prevent people from being distracted by pseudoproblems in thinking. In Wallace's view, the point of theorizing is to solve actual human problems. But he also offers clear proposals about the content of a good life. The primary elements of the view on offer in Wallace's writing are these. A meaningful human life need not be special; it need not be characterized by commitment to values or projects that are unique, unusual, or extreme. There is value in ordinary, everyday, and even seemingly banal experiences. But is there a theory behind all this? What makes these things good for us? Where does his rejection of other theories leave him? And, according to him, are there facts of the matter about human well-being, such that someone could be mistaken about what makes her life go well? Our reading of Wallace will begin to sketch answers to these and other questions.

WALLACE ON IRONISM

In his 1993 essay "E Unibus Pluram: Television and U.S. Fiction," Wallace argues that "irony tyrannizes us."[2] As Wallace traces irony's recent history in America, it gained popularity as a cultural tool for exposing hypocrisy. Irony can purport to show, for example, that institutions commonly promote absurdly idealized images of themselves, that people's claims to represent the interests of others are often self-seeking ploys, and that many traditionally held values are in tension. Irony began its recent popularity as an avant-garde liberator. Later on, says Wallace, it became a culturally entrenched source of unhappiness.

What has this to do with the good life? Wallace sees the pervasiveness of irony in contemporary culture through its impact on television programming. The entertainment industry—one of the early targets of (ironic) postmodern cultural criticism—has hoisted irony's banner. Ironic humor became a staple of television because the market demands it. One of Wallace's examples here is late-night host David Letterman, the "archangel" of contemporary irony. In an interview Wallace remarked: "The particular kind of irony I'm talking about when Letterman comes out and says, 'What a fine crowd,' and everybody roars with laughter, came about in the 60s."[3] Wallace argued that irony and self-consciousness had served crucial and valuable purposes but that "their aesthetic's absorption by U.S. commercial culture has had appalling consequences for writers and everyone else."[4] Viewers enjoy ironic humor about news, gossip, and the like, we surmise, because they understand the ironic point of view, appreciate its presuppositions, regard ironic treatments of various topics as appropriate and smart. In short, viewers think ironically themselves. Or at least aspire to.

But irony is a source of unhappiness, thinks Wallace. Why? And how does irony attract us while making us unhappy? Here's an extended passage from *Infinite Jest* on the loneliness of teenaged Hal Incandenza:

It's of some interest that the lively arts of the millennial U.S.A. treat anhedonia and internal emptiness as hip and cool. It's maybe the vestiges of the Romantic glorification of *Weltschmerz*, which means world-weariness or hip ennui. Maybe it's the fact that most of the arts here are produced by world-weary and sophisticated older people and then consumed by younger people who not only consume art but study it for clues on how to be cool, hip—and keep in mind that, for kids and younger people, to be hip and cool is the same as to be admired and accepted and included and so Unalone. Forget so-called peer-pressure. It's more like peer-*hunger*. No? We enter a spiritual puberty where we snap to the fact that the great transcendent horror is loneliness, excluded encagement in the self. Once we've hit this age, we will now give or take anything, wear any mask, to fit, be part-of, not be Alone, we young. The U.S. arts are our guide to inclusion. A how-to. We are shown how to fashion masks of ennui and jaded irony at a young age where the face is fictile enough to assume the shape of whatever it wears. And then it's stuck there, the weary cynicism that saves us from gooey sentiment and unsophisticated naïveté. Sentiment equals naïveté on this continent.[5]

Irony is appealing, then, not only because adopting an ironic attitude lets us fit in and feel less alone. We also get to present ourselves as being savvy—knowingly bored with the sentimental banalities that others mistakenly value. The mask of ennui we present to others proves we at least aren't naïve.

Wallace goes on to explain why this ironic stance makes us unhappy:

Hal, who's empty but not dumb, theorizes privately that what passes for hip cynical transcendence of sentiment is really some kind of fear of being really human, since to be really human (at least as he conceptualizes it) is probably to be unavoidably sentimental and naïve and goo-prone and generally pathetic, is to be in some basic interior way forever infantile, some sort of not-quite-right-looking infant dragging itself anaclitically around the map, with big wet eyes and froggy-soft skin, huge skull, gooey drool. One of the really American things about Hal, probably, is the way he despises what it is he's really lonely for: this hideous internal self, incontinent of sentiment and need, that pules and writhes just under the hip empty mask, anhedonia.[6]

Wallace's insight on irony is this: when worn as a mask, irony helps one cast a striking figure, but it is privately, personally destructive. It prevents us from doing what human nature pushes us to do: to care about things sincerely and to pursue what we care about. Once in the grip of irony, we are so afraid of appearing really to value things that we turn ironic to the core. We don't value anything at all. Irony is, Wallace writes, "not a rhetorical mode that wears well. . . . This is because irony, entertaining as it is, serves an almost exclusively negative function. It's critical and destructive, a ground-clearing. . . . But irony's singularly unuseful when it comes to constructing anything to replace the hypocrisies it debunks."[7] It leaves human beings empty and isolated, with no way to improve their situation—aside from subjecting themselves to ironic criticism.

Another observer, Richard Rorty, once set down a statement of just the sort of thing Wallace described.[8] Rorty writes:

All human beings carry about a set of words which they employ to justify their actions, their beliefs, and their lives. These are the words in which we formulate praise of our friends and contempt for our enemies, our long-term projects, our deepest self-doubts and our highest hopes. They are the words in which we tell, sometimes prospectively and sometimes retrospectively, the story of our lives. I shall call these words a person's "final vocabulary."[9]

With that terminology in hand, Rorty continues:

I shall define an "ironist" as someone who fulfills three conditions: (1) She has radical and continuing doubts about the final vocabulary she currently uses, because she has been impressed by other vocabularies, vocabularies taken as final by people or books she has encountered; (2) she realizes that argument phrased in her present vocabulary can neither underwrite nor dissolve these doubts; (3) insofar as she philosophizes about her situation, she does not think that her vocabulary is closer to reality than others, that it is in touch with a power not herself.[10]

Insofar as Rorty's ironist can be committed to valuing anything, it is only in a weak sense. The ironist seriously doubts that what she values is really important. Her commitment won't withstand criticism from anyone who rejects it. To defend against such criticism, the ironist has two options. She might shoot back at her critic, charging that he's simply foisting his values on others, as he can't defend his values from outside criticism either. Or the ironist might instead distance herself from the thing she values, confessing that it's not valuable.

But Rorty manages to stay upbeat about the ironist's stance. Rorty argues that a society of ironists can remain committed to humane values by distinguishing between public and private justification. In Rorty's society of ironists, people "would feel no more need to answer the questions 'Why are you a liberal? Why do you *care* about the humiliation of strangers?' than the average sixteenth-century Christian felt to answer the question 'Why are you a Christian?' "[11] But ironists' private stance is another matter. They are "never quite able to take themselves seriously because [they are] always aware that the terms in which they describe themselves are subject to change, always aware of the contingency and fragility of their final vocabularies, and thus of their selves."[12]

It's important to see a difference between Rorty's ironist and Wallace's. The Rortean ironist is "impressed by other vocabularies" and thus seems to have some basis for her ironic intellectual stance. But Wallace's ironist isn't intellectually motivated and, if anything, goes in for ironism because of a desire to be beyond criticism, to be cool. Of course, these approaches to ironism aren't incompatible. Nevertheless, Wallace would not be satisfied with Rorty's positive take on ironism. How we feel about ourselves and our values matters. Hal is not leading a good life. Rorty would point out that Hal can remain publicly committed to caring about the suffering of others. But this is of no consolation to Hal. His private emptiness is a form of suffering, too.

Though irony once had a purpose, Wallace thinks, it became a source of the kind of cruelty it earlier undermined. Wallace's speculation on possible means of irony's removal offers further insight into his views about the good life:

> The next real literary "rebels" in this country might well emerge as some weird bunch of anti-rebels, born oglers who dare somehow to back away from ironic watching, who have the childish gall actually to endorse and instantiate single-entendre principles. Who treat of plain old untrendy human troubles and emotions in U.S. life with reverence and conviction. Who eschew self-consciousness and hip fatigue. These anti-rebels would be outdated, of course, before they even started. Dead on the page. Too sincere. Clearly repressed. Backward, quaint, naïve, anachronistic. Maybe that'll be the point. Maybe that's why they'll be the next real rebels. Real rebels, as far as I can see, risk disapproval. The old postmodern insurgents risked the gasp and squeal: shock, disgust, outrage, censorship, accusations of socialism, anarchism, nihilism. Today's risks are different. The new rebels might be artists willing to risk the yawn, the rolled eyes, the cool smile, the nudged ribs, the parody of gifted ironists, the "Oh how banal." To risk accusations of sentimentality, melodrama. Of overcredulity. Of softness. Of willingness to be suckered by a world of lurkers and starers who fear gaze and ridicule above imprisonment without law.[13]

Wallace clearly thinks that a good life is one of sincere, unironic commitment. But the nature of the commitment and its relationship to value remain unclear. Let's turn to some other thoughts about the good life to look for Wallace's own view.

WALLACE ON HEDONISM

The upshot of the previous section is that Wallace regards sincere commitment to a set of values as a necessary condition for a good human life.

What particular values might someone be sincerely committed to? For starters, whatever is valuable makes a life go well. Everyone will grant that things like food, shelter, and good books can be valuable when they are a means to some further value. But what's ultimately, noninstrumentally valuable? What is good in and of itself? Unsurprisingly, there is no agreement among philosophers, here as elsewhere.[14] One perennial answer, endorsed by thinkers from Epicurus to Jeremy Bentham, is called *value hedonism*. The basic idea is that having pleasure is what makes life go well.[15]

What would Wallace make of value hedonism? He would be unequivocally hostile to one brand of hedonism, it seems. Some hedonists say that pleasure is a favorable attitude toward an experienced state of affairs. According to these theorists, what makes pleasure valuable is not the feeling or sensation itself, but our enjoyment of the sensation. It's the *attitude of enjoyment* that is crucial. That attitude, say these theorists, is what has value. By contrast, other hedonists think of pleasure purely as a sensation. They say that the valuable thing about pleasure is the sensation itself—immediate sensory experiences themselves are good. On this understanding of pleasure, someone may enjoy some experience of hers, but it's not her enjoyment of the experience that gives it value.

Wallace sees pleasure-as-mere-sensation hedonism as an unacceptably narrow account of the good human life. Consider *Infinite Jest*, in which several characters become fixated on the film of the same title. Watching that film is so blissful that viewers can't tear themselves away, and they eventually die after ignoring all other areas of life. Wallace's case is complicated.[16] Yet surely these characters, whatever else we say about them, are not flourishing human beings—even though they satisfy the requirements for flourishing set down by the version of hedonism at issue. Or consider what Wallace says in his essay about a seven-night luxury Caribbean cruise: he reflects on the "Insatiable Infant" part of himself, the part that "WANTS" felt pleasure. The "big lie" of the luxury cruise, Wallace tells us, is that this infantile part can be finally put to rest by total, perfectly delivered pampering and pleasure. That's a lie because trying to satisfy this infant is impossible—"its whole essence or dasein or whatever lies in its *a priori* insatiability."[17]

But here's a perhaps more straightforward example, drawn from *Infinite Jest*. Prince Q—, the Saudi Minister of Home Entertainment, organizes his life around eating the freshest available Töblerone chocolate bars in immense quantities. The prince's chocolate habit badly imbalances his diet, and he employs a medical attaché to relieve the suffering his diet causes, allowing him to continue eating. The case is amusing, in a way, because the attaché is hired not to treat the addiction but to enable the prince's absurd and unhealthy habit.[18]

One potential reaction to this case—one suggested by pleasure-as-mere-sensation hedonism—is to wish that Prince Q— didn't need to endure such maxillofacial suffering to reach chocolaty bliss. But of course this response misses the point. What's sad here is not only the lengths the prince goes to get pleasure but the narrowness of his life. The problem is not that he doesn't have enough pleasure in life. It's that he has nothing else. His life is about the wrong thing, we think Wallace would say, and so any theory that implies that such a life of pleasure goes well can't be correct.

But Wallace might still seriously entertain other forms of hedonism. What the remaining views share is simple: they allow that the content of well-being is, somehow, "up to us." Hedonism says it's pleasure that matters. On this view, value is "nonobjective," in the sense that what is valuable is determined by how we feel rather than by facts independent of how we feel.[19]

Could Wallace endorse some version of hedonism? There's at least some evidence that he could be friendly to such a view. Following his takedown of ironism in "E Unibus Pluram," he privately expressed interest in the idea that people "construct" value. D. T. Max calls attention to a snippet from Wallace's notebook: "Hyperc[onsciousness] makes life meaningless [. . .]: but what of will to construct OWN meaning? Not the world that gives us meaning but vice versa? Dost[oevski] embodies this—Ellis, Leyner, Leavitt, Franzen, Powers—they do not. Their fictions reduce to complaints and self-pity."[20]

Wallace greatly admired Dostoevsky's boldness in constructing meaning.[21] To construct meaning, let's say, is to produce a kind of value where once there was none. Hedonism suggests a way in which we might produce value: when someone finds pleasure in something, it becomes valuable for her, even if no one previously found pleasure in it and it was thus never valuable before.

We suspect Wallace would agree that some versions of hedonism capture something important. They avoid the ironist's error of never taking herself seriously. In fact, if people do not regard themselves as valuable—indeed, as sources of value—they couldn't care about enjoying anything in the first place. And so hedonism implies that ironism is false. That's a promising start.

Although Wallace would laud value hedonists for sticking out their necks and saying that life should be about something, he nevertheless expresses deep worries about the role of pleasure in a good life. Consider a series of questions from his "Joseph Frank's Dostoevsky":[22]

> Is the real point of my life simply to undergo as little pain and as much pleasure as possible? My behavior sure seems to indicate that this is what I believe, at least a lot of the time. But isn't this kind of a selfish way to live? Forget selfish—isn't it awful lonely? ... But if I decide to decide there's a different, less selfish, less lonely point to my life, won't the reason for this decision be my desire to be less lonely, meaning to suffer less overall pain? Can the decision to be less selfish ever be anything other than a selfish decision?[23]

Wallace wonders here whether hedonism is avoidable as a psychological doctrine—after all, we can always describe the motivation for an action in terms of its expected utility for the actor. But the element of this passage we want to underline is Wallace's recognition that, fully bracketing the apparent selfishness involved in a life of pursuing one's desires, such a life just seems sad. Not only would we say that such a person is selfish, but we'd say that they miss something important about life.

Hedonism grants the individual a kind of license or control over the content of a good life. Yet these views lead to an impoverished account of *why* the chosen content is valuable. Wallace says that life thus described sounds "lonely." We surmise he means that it offers a sad description of states of affairs involving other people. On these theories, other people are no more than *mere objects* in the state of affairs you value. If a friend is valuable to you, why is that? Well, she's valuable because of the pleasure she brings you or the pain she helps you avoid. A friend can be no more than an instrument for your purposes, with respect to matters of value. Unsurprisingly, Wallace thinks this description of friendship seems lonely.

Hedonists won't give up so easily. They may insist that Wallace is confused about their position—it tells us what is good *for* a particular human being. And surely, they'll reply, other people are only good *for someone* to the extent that others serve as useful objects in beneficial states of affairs. Fair enough. But Wallace suggests an explanation for any appeal of this reply.

Everything in my own immediate experience supports my deep belief that I am the absolute center of the universe, the realest, most vivid and important person in existence. We rarely think about this sort of natural, basic self-centeredness, because it's so socially repulsive, but it's pretty much the same for all of us, deep down. It is our default setting, hardwired into our boards at birth. Think about it: there is no experience you have had that you are not the absolute center of. The world as you experience it is there in front of you or behind you, to the left or right of you, on your TV, or your monitor, or whatever. Other people's thoughts and feelings have to be communicated to you somehow, but your own are so immediate, urgent, *real*. You get the idea. But please don't worry that I'm getting ready to preach to you about compassion or other-directedness or all the so-called "virtues." This is not a matter of virtue—it's a matter of my choosing to do the work of somehow altering or getting free of my natural, hardwired default setting which is to be deeply and literally self-centered, and to see and interpret everything through this lens of self.[24]

Wallace thinks that we should reject this way of thinking of the good life. It seems selfish, to be sure,[25] but his point is different: our own natural self-centeredness leads us to *misunderstand* our own good. We confuse the immediacy of our subjective experience with its importance.

If our native viewpoint easily confuses us about what's important, what can be done? Is there another perspective that allows us to think more clearly about value? We will consider one important possibility next.

WALLACE ON NARRATIVE THEORIES OF THE GOOD LIFE

Although Wallace was at least attracted to the idea that we somehow "construct" values that contribute to well-being, hedonism won't fit with his thinking. But there are other ways we might "construct" the content of the good life for ourselves. One family of views is so-called *narrative theories* of the good life. Galen Strawson sums up the core of these theories as follows: "a richly narrative outlook on one's life is essential to living well."[26] The basic idea is that someone has a good life *only if* she has a narrative outlook on her life. To use ordinary terms, she must see her life as making sense as a single story in which she is the main character. Strawson's summing up leaves room for elaboration, and the details are filled in variously by different theorists. Narrative theories have enjoyed some popularity among contemporary philosophers, and prominent advocates include Christine Korsgaard, Charles Taylor, and J. David Velleman.[27]

All narrative theorists affirm that *having a narrative is a necessary condition for a good life*. We'll call this the "weak" thesis. But some theorists also endorse a more controversial thesis according to which *a person simply is the thing described by a narrative*. This "strong" thesis happens to imply the weak thesis, but the latter doesn't imply the former.[28] We will first discuss the weak thesis before we explain how the strong thesis plays a role in one defense of narrative theories.

Narrative theories, like hedonism, allow the content of someone's good to be determined by particular features of her psychology. Consider how narrative theories leave value "up to us" in a sense while avoiding some pitfalls of hedonism. For one thing, the value of elements within our stories may depend on various propositional attitudes, and those are certainly not limited to the attitude of enjoyment. For another, the potential roles of persons—ourselves included—within our stories is less restrictive. On narrative theories, persons are characters just as in literature, playing far more nuanced roles than self as enjoyer-of-states-of-affairs or friend as instrument-in-bringing-about-enjoyable-states-of-affairs. Hedonism would seem to recommend analyzing all roles in those limited ways.

Here are two further advantages that narrative theories may enjoy over hedonism. First, narrative theories better capture the richness of human lives and the distinctive value of our long-term projects. For instance, we care about being loving parents, faithful friends, about the success of our work, and so on. Narrative theories allow for a clear divide between these important projects and ephemeral ones. How well our lives go depends on those significant projects, not on whether we clip our fingernails perfectly. Life goes no worse for us, not one bit, when we don't clip our nails right. But, arguably, hedonism must count a poor nail-clipping job as relevant to how our lives go, insofar as such events have some slight impact on our enjoyment. Second, narratives can focus attention in morally significant ways. A person may regard being a faithful friend as an element of her own good, and think that this part of her story is more important than whether she always gets her way in small or trivial matters. So, narratives can redirect our thoughts away from the flow of our first-person experience, precisely as Wallace counsels in *This Is Water*. Stories can guard us against being enslaved by our immediate inclinations.

Parts of *This Is Water* seem to suggest that Wallace may find something to like about narrative theories. One commentator on Wallace's ethical thought has argued that Wallace appreciated "the importance of the direction of attention, and the terms in which we choose to conceive of situations, in our moral lives."[29] Our petty frustration in rush-hour traffic or in a supermarket checkout line may be managed, Wallace thinks, with help from imaginative storytelling. Telling stories about the meaning of commonplace situations may help us overcome our self-centered perspective: we need a narrative that will sympathetically reveal to us the reality of others' lives.[30]

So, narratives refocus the subject of our attention and capture the complexity of our lives and projects. But are stories related to value, according to Wallace? And if so, how? Does he accept some version of narrative theory? Do stories help us lead good lives because a life can't go well without a story?

Wallace seems to deny that well-being requires a narrative outlook.[31] The main question to ask is this: is seeing your life as a story an essential part of a good life? Narrative theorists say "yes," but Wallace answers "no," and we can see this by surveying important passages from his fiction. So, Wallace rejects the weak thesis.

Briefly, before we work through several examples from his fiction, it's worth noting a general theme raised by the examples: narratives increase self-awareness and so prompt us to ask ourselves questions that tend to undermine well-being. Here are the kinds of questions we have in mind: *Am I living up to my own idea of myself? Does my story have the virtues of good stories? Is it original, unique? Are there no unnecessary or dull sections? Is this a story other people will like? Are they interested? Does my concern with these questions really reveal that, down deep, I'm committed to this narrative for the wrong reasons to begin with?* It's one thing to lean back from the steady flow of the first-person perspective, which Wallace recommends, and another altogether to become hyper-self-aware in that way. Someone might end up feeling cramped or even tyrannized by thinking about one's narrative. Indeed, Wallace more than once reveals how asking these sorts of questions can undermine a person's well-being.

Turn now to some examples. Wallace holds that when someone thinks of her life in terms of her narrative, far from helping her lead a good life, it may make her feel like she has fallen short. She is driven to ask the kind of questions noted earlier about her motivation in choosing her commitments in the first place. The result is what Wallace calls the fraudulence paradox:

> The fraudulence paradox was that the more time and effort you put into trying to appear impressive or attractive to other people, the less impressive or attractive you felt inside—you were a fraud. And the more of a fraud you felt like, the harder you tried to convey an impressive or likable image of yourself so that other people wouldn't find out what a hollow, fraudulent person you really were.[32]

This way of managing appearances leaves the narrator "frightened, lonely, alienated, etc." The problem here is with one's self-perception. Thinking of one's life from the point of view of a narrative makes one self-conscious and, in turn, interferes with living well.

In "The Depressed Person," Wallace offered a distressing look at how self-awareness can literally ruin a life. The story's main character is clinically depressed and fully aware of her condition. Her deep concern is that her depression prevents her from being anything more than a parasite on her friends—her "support system." She'd like to realize her "capacity for basic human empathy and compassion and caring."[33] But how can she do this when she is focused entirely on herself? Paradoxically, concern for her life's narrative fixes her gaze there. In the story, in the wake of her therapist's suicide, the depressed person realizes that she is herself inappropriately self-centered. She expresses concerns about her self-centeredness to a terminally ill friend:

The depressed person shared that the most frightening implication of this (i.e., of the fact that, even when she centered and looked deep within herself, she felt she could locate no real feelings for the therapist as an autonomously valid human being) appeared to be that all her agonized pain and despair since the therapist's suicide had in fact been all and only for herself, i.e. for her loss, her abandonment, her grief, her trauma and pain and primal affective survival. And, the depressed person shared that she was taking the additional risk of revealing, even more frightening, that this shatteringly terrifying set of realizations, instead now of awakening in her any feelings of compassion, empathy, and other-directed grief for the therapist as a person, had—and here the depressed person waited patiently for an episode of retching in the especially available trusted friend to pass so that she could take the risk of sharing this with her— that these shatteringly frightening realizations had seemed, terrifyingly, merely to have brought up and created still more and further feelings in the depressed person about herself. At this point in the sharing, the depressed person took a time-out to solemnly swear to her long-distance, gravely ill, frequently retching but still caring and intimate friend that there was no toxic or pathetically manipulative self-excoriation here in what she (i.e., the depressed person) was reaching out and opening up and confessing, only profound and unprecedented fear: the depressed person was frightened for herself . . . she told the supportive friend with the neuroblastoma. She was asking sincerely, the depressed person said, honestly, desperately: what kind of person could seem to feel nothing—"nothing," she emphasized— for anyone but herself? . . . What words and terms might be applied to describe and assess such a solipsistic, self-consumed, endless emotional vacuum and sponge as she now appeared to herself to be? How was she to decide and describe—even to herself, looking inward and facing herself—what all she'd so painfully learned said about her?[34]

What this passage reveals—excruciatingly—is that the depressed person has a serious problem not only with depression, but with narcissism.[35] The depressed person thinks that living a good life, for her, depends in part on whether she meets her description of a compassionate friend. Wallace helps us see here that narratives don't always get us "out of our own heads" in the right way. Instead of thinking of her terminally ill friend, the depressed person wonders whether she's doing enough to qualify as compassionate. Wallace seems to use compassion to show that concern for narrative interferes with the realization of other-regarding virtue. Because the depressed person's attention is focused on her narrative and whether she's living up to it, her efforts to be compassionate leave her feeling even worse about herself. Any compassionate act pushes her even further from realizing her narrative because she'll have acted to make herself qualify as compassionate, not out of genuine concern for another. Her narrative perspective actually makes it impossible for her to attain her ideal. The narrative makes her feel like a fraud and a failure.

Wallace's fiction also highlights a related problem: we tend to overvalue uniqueness or specialness in narratives, and this leaves us feeling inauthentic. One popular assumption in our culture is that an authentic and valuable life must be characterized by special, unusual, or even extreme commitments. We're relentlessly subjected to the message that everyone is different, and so it seems reasonable for us to conclude that we're living defective lives if we lack eccentric values. But this is to confuse uniqueness with authenticity. The main character in Wallace's "Good Old Neon," Neal, makes precisely that mistake.

I spent all my time trying to get [my peers] to think I was dry and jaded as well. . . . Putting in all this time and energy to create a certain impression and get approval or acceptance that then I felt nothing about because it didn't have anything to do with who I really was inside, and I was disgusted with myself for always being such a fraud, but I couldn't seem to help it. Here are some of the various things I tried: EST, riding a ten-speed to Nova Scotia and back, hypnosis, cocaine, sacro-cervical chiropractic, joining a charismatic church, jogging, pro bono work for the Ad Council, meditation classes, the Masons, analysis, the Landmark Forum, the Course in Miracles, a right-brain drawing workshop, celibacy, collecting and restoring vintage Corvettes, and trying to sleep with a different girl every night for two straight months.[36]

Wallace's suggestion is that Neal felt the need to try out these commitments because they cast him in a certain light for the audience of his narrative. His commitments presented him as kind, cynical and world-weary, spiritually deep, emotionally damaged in some interesting way, or some other mix of special traits. There are at least two clear problems with trying to construct a life narrative that is unique. First, as Wallace later has the narrator remark, "human beings are all pretty much identical in terms of our hardwiring."[37] It's difficult to come up with commitments that make one stand out as a *truly* unique person. Anything that one person finds appealing will probably also appeal to others. Second, and more fundamentally, the uniqueness of a commitment is usually unrelated to its value. A painting or a cantata doesn't become less beautiful as more people enjoy it. The same is true of the narrative elements that might constitute a good life. The things someone cares about might distinguish her from others, but that's not enough, by itself anyway, to make them valuable for her.

Both points find clear expression at the conclusion of "Good Old Neon." In the end, Neal begins to think that the reason he felt like such a fraud, yet was hopeless to change, was that he was unable to love. He couldn't let himself be happy because he couldn't even love himself. Tragically, he applied the criteria for a good narrative even to his diagnosis of why his life wasn't going well, and his explanation proved insufficiently unique.

I happened on part of an old *Cheers* episode from late in the series' run where the analyst character, Frasier . . . , and Lilith, his fiancée and also an analyst, are just entering the stage set of the underground tavern, and Frasier is asking her how her workday at her office went, and Lilith says, "If I have one more yuppie come in and start whining to me about how he can't love, I'm going to throw up." This line got a huge laugh from the show's studio audience, which indicated that they—and so by demographic extension the whole national audience at home as well—recognized what a cliché and melodramatic type of complaint the inability-to-love concept was. . . . The flash of realizing all this at the very same time that the huge audience-laugh showed that nearly everybody in the United States had probably already seen through the complaint's inauthenticity as long ago as whenever the episode had originally run. . . . It more or less destroyed me, that's the only way I can describe it, as if whatever hope of any way out of the trap I'd made for myself had been blasted out of midair or laughed off the stage, as if I were one of those stock comic characters who is always both the butt of the joke and the only person not to get the joke.[38]

The sadness here is palpable. Neal has assumed a good life needs to be unique, though here he finds this can't be true for his own life: he's like many other people. But it shouldn't be surprising that many people have, or think they have, the same problem. And of course the fact that so many people are similarly afflicted does not mean it's insignificant or that they are inauthentic.

The wide distribution of the inability-to-love problem certainly doesn't reveal that someone with this problem would be more authentic were it his alone. Even if the distinctiveness of a problem happened to make some person's story more interesting to an audience, that would have nothing to do with whether his life goes well. Wallace thinks that our culture overvalues uniqueness, and surely he's right.

So far, we have noted examples from Wallace's fiction where fidelity to a narrative undermines well-being. The examples are crucial for understanding Wallace's attitude toward narrative theories.

These cases are counterexamples to the weak thesis—the claim that well-being requires a narrative outlook on life. To illustrate why, consider the narrator in "Good Old Neon." Tear away his life's circumstances from his tangled web of narrative. Here are the facts: Neal has a family who loves him, a knack for interesting work, time to devote to volunteering and hobbies, and so forth. This guy's life appears on track to go well. He's blessed. But notice what happens once we drop him back inside the narrative structure he has built up. There things start to fall apart for him—the narrativity badly screws him up. Because of his story about his own fraudulence and his inability to love, anything valuable in his life now fails to make him better off. The narrative is a kind of poison.

Wallace wants us to see that the narrator's fidelity to his narrative ruins his life. But we must not ignore a corollary: *his life would have been a good one without the narrative.* From this it seems to follow that that narrative is not required for a good life. Wallace's example of narrative undermining well-being casts doubt on the weak thesis. The important question, again: is seeing life as a story an essential part of a good life? Wallace sure seems to think there are cases where that's not so. The same point could be made with the other examples as well, but let's proceed.

Although narrative theorists will no doubt agree that narratives *can* undermine well-being, they may insist that's because the narratives are improperly used, *not* because well-being doesn't require a narrative outlook on life. In light of Wallace's examples, then, narrative theorists might try to explain why narratives sometimes undermine the good life.

A first thought is that Wallace's examples underline problems people tend to encounter by using narratives as action-guiding plans. But using narratives in that way is a mistake. Narratives are not for action guidance—they are for *evaluation* of a life's goodness. This means that a theory of the good life may be "self-effacing"— that is, the good might sometimes be better promoted by ignoring the theory itself—but, for all that, the theory might be true. Many philosophers have been satisfied with self-effacing theories of the good. Though we strongly suspect that Wallace would regard this as undesirable, we'll wait for the conclusion to say more. For now, let's assume that this line is closed off for narrative theorists.

Here's another thought. Defenders of narratives might try to avoid the problems Wallace noted by revising the weak thesis. They might say that narratives undermine well-being in difficult cultural conditions and insist that narratives must be endorsed by someone free of cultural defects. Who? A suitably idealized agent—that is, a fully informed or perfectly rational person. In other words, the narrative theorists would claim that not just any old narrative will do: the weak thesis must be supplemented with more demanding conditions for what sort of narrative can make a life good. Then the weak thesis is transformed as follows: well-being requires *a narrative outlook on life that's also endorsed by a suitably idealized agent.* Plausibly, an idealized agent wouldn't consider features like uniqueness, for instance, in developing a narrative. (For instance, an idealized agent wouldn't experience Neal's embarrassment and self-loathing in response to the joke on *Cheers* because those reactions are based on a mistaken concern for uniqueness.) Thus, sophisticated narrative theories can avoid the problems arising from culture that Wallace points out. Some of Wallace's criticisms are indeed leveled at unhealthy uses of narratives that result from nonideal cultural conditions. But he also raises a deeper point, mentioned in passing above, that tells against the idea that a narrative is necessary for well-being. To judge one's life in terms of narrative success is to adopt a certain perspective. This perspective involves thinking of oneself as a character in a story, and evaluating that character in terms of her or his compliance with the story's demands. If this sounds alienating, there's a good reason. It is. In fact, this very change in perspective gives rise to the paradox of fraudulence that Wallace describes—"that the more time and effort you put into trying to appear impressive or attractive to [an audience], the less impressive or attractive you felt inside."[39] The narrator in "Good Old Neon" describes the attitude to oneself that the narrative perspective calls for:

> In the dream, I was in the town commons in Aurora . . . and what I'm doing in the dream is sculpting an enormous marble or granite statue of myself . . . and when the statue's finally done I put it up on a big bandstand or platform and spend all my time polishing it and keeping birds from sitting on it or doing their business on it, and cleaning up litter and keeping the grass neat all around the bandstand. And in the dream my whole life flashes by like that, the sun and moon go back and forth across the sky like windshield wipers over and over, and I never seem to sleep or eat or take a shower . . . meaning I'm condemned to a whole life of being nothing but a sort of custodian to the statue.[40]

Narrative theories turn us into custodians of ideal selves. But that isn't what being a human being is about, Wallace thinks. After finally being persuaded by the mocking laughter of the *Cheers* studio audience that his fraudulence was inescapable, the narrator, Neal, offers a final diagnosis for his life's failure: "my own basic problem was that at an early age I'd somehow chosen to cast my lot with my life's drama's supposed audience instead of with the drama itself."[41] In requiring us to side with the audience of our narrative and not with ourselves, narrative theories alienate us from who we are and what's good for us. We should experience our lives as participants instead of as spectators.

Some narrative theorists may have an interesting reply to this concern. Let's suppose that our narratives don't merely describe what is good for us. They constitute us. This is the stronger understanding of narrative theory mentioned already—a person is *identical* with her narrative. Christine Korsgaard has defended this idea and writes: "We construct ourselves from our choices, from our actions, from the reasons that we legislate."[42] So, narratives do more than set the parameters for a good life. Narratives also make particular persons who they are. Crucially, if that's so, there can be no complaint about alienation. If you are your narrative, there's no way your narrative can alienate you from yourself. There's no *you* without it.

The strong thesis features a subtle and complicated understanding of the self. We're not ultimately sure how Wallace would engage with the view, but there's one passage in his writings that may serve as a kind of response to it.

Perhaps Wallace would reject this view of the self's constitution because it misconstrues what a person is. To see what we mean, compare the following two passages. Witness Korsgaard on the value of a life in which one violates the commitments of one's narrative:

> It is the conceptions of ourselves that are most important to us that give rise to unconditional obligations. For to violate them is to lose your integrity and so your identity, and to no longer be

who you are. That is, it is to no longer be able to think of yourself under the description under which you value yourself and find your life to be worth living and your actions to be worth undertaking. It is to be for all practical purposes dead or worse than dead.[43]

Compare Korsgaard's words to a striking passage from "Good Old Neon." Wallace is here speaking to the narrator about the narrator's decision to commit suicide, his decision to escape the essential fraudulence that comes with failing to achieve the goals of his various narratives (or even to settle on a single narrative). Wallace addresses the postmortem Neal:

You already know the difference between the size and speed of everything that flashes through you and the tiny inadequate bit of it all you can ever let anyone know. As though inside you is this enormous room full of what seems like everything in the whole universe at one time or another and yet the only parts that get out have to somehow squeeze out through one of those tiny keyholes you see under the knob in older doors. As if we are all trying to see each other through these tiny keyholes. . . . What exactly do you think you are? The millions and trillions of thoughts, memories, juxtapositions . . . that flash through your head and disappear? Some sum or remainder of these? Your *history?* . . . The truth is you've already heard this. That this is what it's like. That it's what makes room for the universes inside you, all the endless inbent fractals of connection and symphonies of different voices, the infinities you can never show another soul. And you think it makes you a fraud, the tiny fraction anyone else ever sees? Of course you're a fraud, of course what people see is never you. And of course you know this, and of course you try to manage what part they see if you know it's only a part. Who wouldn't? It's called free will, Sherlock. But at the same time it's why it feels so good to break down and cry in front of others, or to laugh, or speak in tongues, or chant in Bengali—it's not English anymore, it's not getting squeezed through any hole. So cry all you want, I won't tell anybody. But it wouldn't have made you a fraud to change your mind. It would be sad to do it because you think you somehow have to.[44]

Here's the philosophical point: we are not merely our narratives, Wallace would say, because no narrative—perhaps nothing ever explicitly thought in words—can capture who we are. Although narratives can usefully express to others and to ourselves what we care about, they are never *who we are*. Selves are ineffable.[45]

Korsgaard tells us that people who don't live up to their narratives haven't merely let themselves down—they have chosen a life that amounts to being "dead or worse than dead." Neal tells himself a story according to which he's a fraud, and thinks suicide is his only nonfraudulent option. Wallace appreciates the sadness in this—killing yourself for the sake of your narrative. Which passage, Korsgaard's or Wallace's, sounds more humane?

CONCLUSION

Wallace reflected on human well-being through his fiction and he offered real insights. Here are three. He contends, against the ironist, that our lives should be about something, and that we should not be embarrassed to say so and sincerely mean it. He argues compellingly that a life need not be unique or unusual to be valuable. And he offers reasons to reject the idea that well-being comes solely from pleasure.

Our discussion has been limited to theories on which people construct value, rather than discover it, because of Wallace's apparent preference for such views. But what would he think of so-called *objective list theories* of the good life? Those theories say that certain things—say, relationships and attaining significant knowledge—make our lives go well independently of our thoughts or preferences about them. On the one hand, Wallace might think that these views are guilty of the moralizing he means to avoid.[46] On the other hand, recall Wallace's admiration for Dostoevsky's courage in sticking his neck out and creating meaning.[47] So, we wonder: doesn't it require even greater courage to say that values are *really out there*, no matter what anyone thinks or feels, than it does to say they exist as a product of our constructive activity? We don't know how Wallace comes down on this issue. Perhaps he'd take an intermediate view, on which we construct value without always realizing it, and we gradually discover it within ourselves, often finding that it's at odds with our more conscious self-conceptions. Perhaps value is one part of "the universes inside you" that's ineffable, inexpressible.

We find in Wallace's writing more than piecemeal criticism of other views and a glimpse of bits and pieces of his own. We also find a humane recommendation about how to approach reflection on the good life. It's a sort of Wittgensteinian methodology, for lack of a better term. Wallace's interest in Wittgenstein has been well documented.[48] Wittgenstein famously remarked in *Philosophical Investigations*: "Philosophy is a battle against the bewitchment of our intelligence by means of language."[49] Wallace sees this as a dictum about the point of thinking and about the role of theories in thinking well. Thinking is supposed to solve problems. Thinking about what makes your life go well should not make you worse off.[50]

But some theories do precisely that. If we regard some version of narrative theory as action guiding—if we treat it as a practical guide that gives us reasons to act—then our lives will may go poorly, even by that theory's lights. As Wallace shows, concern about how one's life appears to an audience interferes with living a good life.

Leading a good life calls for a level of involvement with the action that's precluded by too much self-awareness. Some theorists have said that their views are self-effacing, as we noted above. Their theories set out standards for evaluating lives, not guides for how to live. If we look to such theories to provide motives for acting, our lives go poorly.

One standard complaint with particular moral theories is that they're self-effacing. Wallace sees the problem as being more widespread—it's endemic to theories of the good life. The ingredients for human well-being are too subtle to be represented in a theory or, indeed, in language. Attempts to theorize about value result in partial and distorted vision. An important metaphor from "Good Old Neon" is instructive on Wallace's view, we think:

> The ground fog tends to get more intense by the second until it seems that the whole world is just what's in your headlights' reach. High beams don't work in fog, they only make things worse. You can go ahead and try them but you'll see what happens, all they do is light up the fog so it seems even denser. That's kind of a minor paradox, that sometimes you can actually see farther with low beams than high.[51]

All of us sometimes get confused about what would be good for us, about what matters, or about what matters most. Theories refocus our attention and offer answers. Sometimes, we need a helping hand: our natural inclinations are imperfect guides to what matters in life. But following theories is risky. Theories redescribe values so they'll fit within theories—or, sometimes worse, theories explain particular values away entirely. They turn simple matters, ones we could see through perfectly fine, into intellectual perplexities. We can figure out some things—like the value of relationships or the proper expression of compassion—better without theories. None of this means that theories of the good life are bad or useless. They just need to be kept in their place. We need to recognize what such theories are for.

So what are they for? One proposal, borrowed from David Schmidtz, is that theories are best understood as maps: "A map is not itself the reality," writes Schmidtz. "It is at best a serviceable representation. Moral theories likewise are more or less serviceable representations of a terrain. They cannot be more than that."[52] Different problems call for different maps, and we know that a map won't tell us everything. It shouldn't, either. A map that details everything about its subject is useless, in part because we don't need the map to represent everything, and we can't use everything anyhow. Maps are only helpful when we need to know the way. They sometimes work as stand-ins for practical wisdom about the local terrain. But they are never good when treated as full-scale reproductions of the world.

With these points in mind, notice that Wallace can answer the claim that a theory might be true but self-effacing: it's not much of a theory if it can't tell us how to go somewhere we need to go. Determining whether or not a life was good, after the fact, is usually not a genuine human problem. A theory that could offer us the correct answer to that question would be an intellectual achievement, to be sure, but Wallace sees it as little else. The point of thinking is to solve problems that matter to us, not to be clever for cleverness's sake.

Kurt Baier once complained that "moral talk is often rather repugnant. Leveling moral accusations, expressing moral indignation, passing moral judgment, allotting the blame, administering moral reproof, justifying oneself, and, above all, moralizing—who can enjoy such talk?"[53] When we talk about or apply a moral view, it might seem judgmental or cruel to others. But there is another way a moral theory might be cruel. Wallace recognizes that theories of the good life, when taken to be more than limited sketches of reality, tend to result in our being judgmental or cruel *to ourselves.* Our pursuit of good in life is about something else entirely, thinks Wallace:

> If you can think of times in your life that you've treated people with extraordinary decency and love, and pure uninterested concern, just because they were valuable as human beings. The ability to do that with ourselves. To treat ourselves the way we would treat a really good, precious friend. Or a tiny child of ours that we absolutely loved more than life itself. And I think it's probably possible to achieve that. I think part of the job we're here for is to learn how to do this.[54]

NOTES

This paper is the product of full and equal collaboration between its authors. The authors wish to express their gratitude to Andrew Bailey, Thomas Crisp, William Dyer, Chris Freiman, Stephen Grimm, David Schmidtz, David Storey, and Benjamin Wilson for comments on an earlier version of this essay.

1. David Foster Wallace, interview by Larry McCaffery, "An Interview with David Foster Wallace," *Review of Contemporary Fiction* 13, no. 2 (summer 1993): 131.
2. David Foster Wallace, "E Unibus Pluram: Television and U.S. Fiction," in *A Supposedly Fun Thing I'll Never Do Again* (New York: Little, Brown and Company, 1997), 67.
3. See Stephen J. Burn, ed., *Conversations with David Foster Wallace* (Jackson: University Press of Mississippi, 2012), 80.
4. McCaffery, "An Interview," 146.
5. David Foster Wallace, *Infinite Jest* (New York: Little, Brown and Company, 1996), 694.
6. Wallace, *Infinite Jest*, 694–695.
7. Wallace, "E Unibus Pluram," 67.
8. Wallace was certainly aware of Rorty—one of Rorty's books is the namesake of Wallace's story "Philosophy and the Mirror of Nature." We wonder: had Wallace read Rorty's work on irony? If so, was he influenced by it?

9. Richard Rorty, *Contingency, Irony, and Solidarity* (Cambridge: Cambridge University Press, 1989), 73.
10. Ibid.
11. Ibid., 87.
12. Ibid., 73–74.
13. Wallace, "E Unibus Pluram," 81–82. For more on similar themes, see Wallace's essay "Robert Frank's Dostoevsky," in *Consider the Lobster and Other Essays* (New York: Little, Brown and Company, 2005). Wallace regards Dostoevsky as a writer who exemplified the "brave" unironic commitment to "moral/spiritual values."
14. See Shelly Kagan, *Normative Ethics* (Boulder, Colo.: Westview, 1998), 29–41, for a brief review of accounts of well-being. See also Russ Shafer-Landau, *The Fundamentals of Ethics*, 2nd ed. (New York: Oxford University Press, 2011), chaps. 1–4, for discussion of hedonism and the desire-satisfaction theory.
15. We'll only consider Wallace's reactions to hedonism here, but we think that Wallace would take a similar stance toward a related "nonobjective" view, the desire-satisfaction theory of well-being, according to which having one's desires satisfied, getting what one wants, makes life go well, whether it's pleasurable or not.
16. It's at least superficially like Robert Nozick's "experience machine." See his *Anarchy, State, and Utopia* (New York: Basic Books, 1974), 42–45.
17. Wallace, "A Supposedly Fun Thing I'll Never Do Again," in *A Supposedly Fun Thing*, 316–317.
18. "The medical attaché's particular expertise is the maxillofacial consequences of imbalances in intestinal flora. Prince Q— (as would anyone who refuses to eat pretty much anything but Töblerone) suffers chronically from Candida albicans, with attendant susceptibilities to monilial sinusitis and thrush, the yeasty sores and sinal impactions of which require almost daily drainage" (*Infinite Jest*, 33). Stories like the prince's are not so uncommon in real life. Consider one such story from the history of rock and roll. When Slash, lead guitarist of Guns N' Roses, began regularly passing out in public because of his alcohol and drug abuse, he didn't get help for addiction: he hired a handler to ensure that he didn't get arrested.
19. This view is highly similar to the desire-satisfaction accounts of well-being mentioned in note 15, above.
20. D. T. Max, *Every Love Story Is a Ghost Story* (New York: Penguin, 2013), 209.

21. The passage from Wallace's notebook continues with praise for the Russian writer: "Dostoevski has BALLS."
22. I.e., "really urgent stuff inside asterisks as part of some multivalent defamiliarization-flourish" (Wallace, "Joseph Frank's Dostoevsky," 271).
23. Ibid., 261–262.
24. David Foster Wallace, *This Is Water* (New York: Little, Brown and Company, 2009), 36–44. Wallace is eager to distance himself from morality and moralizing in *This Is Water*: "None of this is about morality, or religion, or dogma, or big fancy questions of life after death" (128). But we think he's interested here in the good life. Daniel Turnbull offers helpful suggestions to explain Wallace's reluctance to call his purposes "moral," even though they are decidedly moral. See Daniel Turnbull, "*This Is Water* and the Ethics of Attention: Wallace, Murdoch, and Nussbaum," in *Consider David Foster Wallace: Critical Essays*, ed. David Hering (Los Angeles: Slide Show Media Group Press, 2010), 210–211.
25. Even if a charge of selfishness reveals the moral wrongness of pursuing our own good at a cost to others, it doesn't show that these accounts of the good are incoherent. After all, it may be that our own good conflicts with the good of others.
26. Galen Strawson, "Narrativity and Non-Narrativity," *Wiley Interdisciplinary Reviews: Cognitive Science* 1, no. 6 (2010): 775. Strawson's paper offers a helpful overview of narrative theories, along with some criticisms.
27. Here is Charles Taylor: "Because we cannot but orient ourselves to the good, and thus determine our place relative to it and hence determine the direction of our lives, we must inescapably understand our lives in narrative form, as a 'quest.' But one could perhaps start from another point: because we have to determine our place in relation to the good, therefore we cannot be without an orientation to it, and hence must see our life in story. From whichever direction, I see these conditions as connected facets of the same reality, inescapable structural requirements of human agency" (Charles Taylor, *Sources of the Self: The Making of the Modern Identity* [Cambridge, Mass.: Harvard University Press, 1989], 51–52).
28. That's because if persons are constituted by narratives, as the strong thesis holds, then there is no *life* to go well or ill minus a narrative. In other words, someone can have a good life only if she has a narrative because she has a *life* only if she has a narrative. But the weak thesis

could be true even if the strong one is false: even if persons are not constituted by narratives, well-being may still require a narrative.

29. Turnbull, "*This Is Water* and the Ethics of Attention," 209.

30. Wallace, *This Is Water*, 77–93.

31. We suspect that Wallace was attracted to narrative theories early in his literary career. For example, his first novel was inspired in part by a girlfriend's remark that she "would rather be a character in a novel than a real person," and Wallace "got to wondering just what the difference was" (Max, *Every Love Story Is a Ghost Story*, 44). (Of course, if there is no difference, the strong thesis is true.) In a 1988 essay, he remarked: "Each drama has a hero. He's purposely designed so that we by our nature 'identify' with him. At present this is still not hard to get us to do, for we still tend to think of our own lives this way: we're each the hero of our own drama, others around us remanded to supporting roles or (increasingly) audience status" (David Foster Wallace, "Fictional Futures and the Conspicuously Young," in *Both Flesh and Not* [New York: Little, Brown, 2012], 50). Though Wallace never says that we should regard our lives as stories or that we must do so to have good lives, he may have thought something like that. Later, as we will see, Wallace came to think that by understanding your life as a kind of narrative, you demote yourself to "audience status," too.

32. David Foster Wallace, "Good Old Neon," in *Oblivion: Stories* (New York: Little, Brown and Company, 2004), 147.

33. David Foster Wallace, "The Depressed Person," in *Brief Interviews with Hideous Men* (New York, Little, Brown and Company, 1999), 57.

34. Ibid., 56–58.

35. That isn't to say that the depressed person's narcissism and depression are unrelated. Wallace briefly discussed the story in an interview: "This is the most painful story I have ever written. It's about the narcissism which accompanies depression. The main figure is marked by my own character traits. I actually lost friends while I was working on this story—I was ugly and unhappy and just yelled at everyone. The terrible thing about depression is that it's such a self-absorbed illness—Dostoyevsky shows this well in his *Notes from the Underground*. Depression is painful—you're devoured by yourself; the worse the depression is, the more you think only of yourself and the more alien and repellent you appear to others." The full interview, in German, is available here:

http://www.zeit.de/2007/05/L-Interview. Thanks to Robin Litscher for
the English translation.

36. Wallace, "Good Old Neon," 142–143.
37. Ibid., 174.
38. Ibid., 168–169.
39. Ibid., 147.
40. Ibid., 160–161.
41. Ibid., 176.
42. Christine Korsgaard, *Self-Constitution: Agency, Identity, and Integrity* (New York: Oxford University Press, 2009), 207.
43. Christine Korsgaard, *Sources of Normativity* (New York: Cambridge University Press, 1996), 102.
44. Wallace, "Good Old Neon," 178–180.
45. Here's a sobering thought or two. All of us are sometimes wrong about ourselves in important ways. We misinterpret our own motives, misunderstand the things that matter to us, and misread our relationships with others. Our lives are often improved when we see these mistakes and try to fix them. But the narrative perspective makes such changes harder than they might otherwise be. It encourages us to ignore or explain away "data" about ourselves that doesn't fit with our current self-conception. It makes facing up to these conflicts into a kind of failure to live up to our story. Narrativity leads us to find linearity in life where it does not always exist. This is no way to understand who we are.
46. See note 24.
47. See the section "Wallace on Hedonism," above.
48. D. T. Max, *Every Love Story Is a Ghost Story*, 44–47. See also Ira B. Nadel, "Consider the Footnote," in *The Legacy of David Foster Wallace*, ed. Samuel Cohen and Lee Konstantinou (Iowa City: University of Iowa Press, 2012), 222–223.
49. Ludwig Wittgenstein, *Philosophical Investigations*, 3rd ed., trans. G. E. M. Anscombe (Malden, Mass.: Blackwell, 2001), 40, §109.
50. The idea here is not that you should accept the theory that yields the most glowing assessment of your own life. Rather, it's that the act of thinking should not make you worse off. To be sure, thinking might well lead you to understand that your life goes badly. That's importantly different than thinking actually causing your life to go worse.
51. Wallace, "Good Old Neon," 177.

52. David Schmidtz, *Elements of Justice* (New York: Cambridge University Press, 2006), 22. We see some parallels between Wallace's view and those Schmidtz develops in his essay "The Meanings of Life," in *Robert Nozick*, ed. D. Schmidtz (New York: Cambridge University Press, 2002).

53. Kurt Baier, *The Moral Point of View: A Rationalist Basis of Ethics*, abridged ed. (New York: McGraw-Hill College, 1965), 3.

54. David Foster Wallace, interview by David Lipsky, in *Although of Course You End Up Becoming Yourself: A Road Trip with David Foster Wallace* (New York: Broadway, 2010), 292–293.

CONTRIBUTORS

STEVEN M. CAHN is professor of philosophy at the Graduate Center of the City University of New York.

MAUREEN ECKERT is associate professor of philosophy at the University of Massachusetts, Dartmouth.

WILLIAM HASKER is professor emeritus of philosophy at Huntington College.

GILA SHER is professor of philosophy at the University of California, San Diego.

M. ORESTE FIOCCO is associate professor of philosophy at the University of California, Irvine.

DANIEL R. KELLY is assistant professor of philosophy at Purdue University.

NATHAN BALLANTYNE is assistant professor of philosophy at Fordham University.

JUSTIN TOSI is a doctoral candidate at the University of Arizona.

INDEX